Pra

Withou

M000267138

"*Without a Net* is the self portrait of a witty bad boy with a heart of gold, a seeker of truth and an adventurer who grabbed my heart and still intrigues me. That's why I married him."

— **Reagan Wilson,** Vintage Playboy Playmate, Miss October 1967

"Compelling and unapologetically honest, Mr. Hornig's memoir is a fascinating read. From New York penthouses to Afghan bazaars and Spanish prisons, from ruin to redemption, *Without a Net* is a real page turner. For sheer entertainment value and great conversation, Barry Hornig has surfaced to the top of my list of "People I'd Most Like To Have Dinner With!"

— **Gail Ranstrom,** Author

"Barry Hornig knows both the mean streets of New York and the terrorist controlled wadis of Afghanistan. A world traveller and adventurer since his early 20's, he survived near death in a notorious Spanish prison, numerous clashes with heavily armed pimps in Manhattan, and almost lost his soul in sado-masochistic subterranean pleasure caves in Gotham's sordid Chelsea district. During the years he coked and danced the night away in Manhattan's fabled Studio 54, he also found time to marry an Italian countess. Travel along with Hornig, as he turns his life around, finding redemption through meditation and contemplation...just in time!"

— **Stephen M. Joseph,** author of *The Shark Bites Back*

"Barry Hornig's book will take you from normalcy to grandeur, to adventure, to squalor, and back again at supersonic speed. There are many authors in the world, but how many have lived it? A great mind can be a curse. This is one man's quest to harness brilliance and the cost of it. A rollicking and raucous journey to nirvana!"

— **Barry Denton,** writer and photographer

"Barry finally heeded that often-heard suggestion from others: "Dude! You should write a book!"

What a memoir and what a memory, describing the who, what, wheres and whens during a whirlwind of moments and times most of us are familiar with – only thing, Barry's lived them, breathed them and totally consumed them, all while balancing himself on that high wire act called life. *Forrest Gump* was a great work of fiction, yet *Without a Net* describes a real-life adventure featuring a kid from Brooklyn who from the get-go went full throttle and pushed down the pedal to the metal.

Barry was in the mix, rubbing elbows with household names, icons from celebrity to notorious. Once Barry Hornig got on a roll he either couldn't, or never wanted to slam on the brakes!

Call it what you want, Barry's *Without a Net* takes us on a sometimes disjointed but always delicious and shameless romp."

– **Lou Christine,** author of *Kill 'em with Kindness*
http://louchristine.com/

"Barry Hornig's *Without A Net* is an unmistakably modern American memoir of the highs and lows of a voyager of the 1960s whose luck shifted multiple times as he sought wealth, adventure and sexual exaltation in a range of places. The narrative has elements of comedy and despair, triumph and failure, but his good-natured storytelling captures personalities and events very close to an American grain many of us lived and loved. A worthy read, and I highly recommend it."

— **William Pearlman**, Author and Playwright

"Barry's book, full of every high and low someone could pack into life in the last half of the 20th Century, is fun and riveting. We follow the cyclone of Barry's journey through the disco days of New York to the hipper than hip scene of Hollywood, when there were still real movie studios. A tale of sex, drugs, rock 'n roll, swimming pools and movie stars. A great snapshot of a wild and wonderful time, if you made it out alive, and Barry did just that, with style and grace."

— **J. Dulin Jones**, Screenwriter and Playwright

"Barry Hornig has lived a life of dreams and nightmares. Fortunately, he learned to tell the difference. Explosive, compelling reading."

— **David Dunham**, Publisher

To my spirit guides;
to my soulmate, Diana;
and to my parents, Willy and Sally.

Without a Net:
A True Tale of Prison, Penthouses and Playmates

by Barry Hornig and
Michael Claibourne

ISBN   978-163393-076-6

Published by

◄ köehlerbooks™

210 60th Street
Virginia Beach, VA 23451
212-574-7939
www.koehlerbooks.com

Handwritten: Santa Monika · *9/30/2017* · *To Mark & Mimi* · *It's so ever forever!!*

Without a Net

A true tale of prison, penthouses and playmates

Barry Hornig
& Michael Claibourne

Handwritten signature: Michael Claibourne

VIRGINIA BEACH
CAPE CHARLES

Table of Contents

Prologue

I should have known what my life was going to be like from early on because I loved the *Cyclone* on Coney Island. Even as a kindergartener, I would drag my grandma and grandpa and anybody else I could hustle or trick into going with me (they wouldn't let little kids on alone), and I would always put them in the rear car, the most dangerous one. My grandparents hated it. But I would make them go on every ride. They were Eastern European and very kind, so they put up with it.

This was advertised as the scariest ride in the world, but I was fearless. I loved it when it was completely dark, and you'd clatter up the track to the top of a hill, and on a clear night you could see the New York City skyline and the lights of the Rockaways. I couldn't get enough of it, while I fortified myself with hot dogs, French fries, and Cokes from the original Nathan's.

After the ride I wandered off to the carnie booths and watched all the bearded men, tattooed ladies, and double-headed people. I couldn't know at the time what a foreshadowing that was of the freak show that would become my life.

I was banned from supermarkets at the age of four. I liked to pull everything down from the racks and scream.

My family lived in my grandma's house in Brooklyn. There was a wonderful girl who would walk me in my stroller up and down in front of the house. And the other day, when I saw on

TV that she had died, I felt very sad. Her name was Suzanne Pleshette. She lived next door, and she was my babysitter.

We moved to Long Beach, on Long Island, in the path of huge storms. I remember my first hurricane and how the house shook. And riding my bike through the streets where the ocean met the bay. There were whitecaps in them.

My dad, who I called Willy, would take me out on a rowboat in Reynolds Channel to fish for flounder and fluke. We ate delicious tuna-fish and salami sandwiches while we fished, but I didn't know, until years later, that he couldn't swim. How brave, and how reckless. A rickety little boat, a big guy with his son... one wrong move, and over the boat goes. He was quite a guy, with his Errol Flynn moustache. I remember going down to the recreation center and watching him and my uncle hit a hard, black handball with gloves. I tried it, and I cried because it hurt my hand.

Every Saturday and Sunday mornings we would go to the beach at eight and stay until dark. My father taught me how to surf-cast and dig for crabs, clams, and starfish. My mother and my aunt would show up by lunchtime with sandwiches and cold watermelon, and my friends and I would swim, fish, and make drippy sand castles.

One afternoon, I went on a walkabout and got lost. In those days, the lifeguards would put a lost child up on a wooden platform and blow the whistle, so their parents would come and claim them. But I had wandered too far off, and they couldn't hear the whistle. I spent an enjoyable afternoon with the lifeguards, but later in the day, my parents found me. They were very unhappy, and I got my first spanking.

My grade school was right around the corner from our new house. The first afternoon I went, I got into a scuffle with somebody and wound up facing the blackboard on a stool with a pointed hat on my head.

I remember my first fight clearly. One of the toughest kids in school was Johnny, who was a little bigger than everybody else, mean, and pushed everybody around. He grabbed me one day and told me he needed money to buy egg creams at the corner store and started to go through my pockets. I don't think I was more than seven or eight, but I stepped back and hit him as hard as I could in the stomach. To my delight, he went down like a sack of rocks. Right to the ground, and he started crying.

I found my new power, and a new way to negotiate.

I had trouble in my early schooling; I am dyslexic, and it was difficult for me to concentrate, so I was a *C* student. A coach helped me study phonetics because all the words looked backwards. I have always had a lot of trouble reading out loud, so, as a kid, I avoided it. I can comprehend language very well when reading to myself.

Although I've never been tested, I think I'm probably bipolar as well. My ups and downs have always been intense, and when I got manic, I was out on the street.

Since the bay and the ocean were only separated by six blocks, we spent most of our time on the water. There were fishing piers, and my friends had small boats, so we went boating up and down the channels after school. In the summer, we had the ocean and the Boardwalk.

I kept out of trouble, even though I was in rumbles and gang fights as I got older, because I was a promising athlete in constant training. I lifted weights and didn't smoke or drink. I had coaches to motivate me from elementary school on—and I was disciplined.

I had my heroes. I watched some of the star athletes in sporting events when I was younger, and it made a great impression on me. I wanted to be the Indian who became an Olympian in the Burt Lancaster movie, *Jim Thorpe—All-American*. I used that film as my blueprint and decided I would never get in trouble, as I was determined to become a fearless athlete with lightning reflexes. I had no qualms about flying through the air or hurting someone in sports. In fact, I wanted to inflict pain; that was my job—to stop the other athletes.

I never realized just how fast I was until they timed me, and I noticed that nobody could beat me. Some of the other kids hated that I was as fast as they all were. I raced with Bobby Frankel on a bet, and won—and he was the fastest boy in Far Rockaway High School and also a Hall of Fame horse trainer. I shot baskets with my friend, Larry Brown. It got to where they wouldn't let Larry shoot any more at carnivals because he won all the teddy bears. Larry became a pro basketball star, and a Hall of Fame coach.

When I went into the city with my buddy, Steady Eddie, we saw street jesters, poets, drifters, and grifters on 42nd Street where we went to the movies—porn movies they didn't show in Long Beach. By the time I was ready to go to college, I was street-smart. I was tall and athletic; people said I was good looking. I always worked so I could help my parents, and I knew everyone on the corner. I was able to inflict pain and run so fast that nobody could catch me. I thought I was special, and I knew I could take care of myself.

That didn't prove to be enough for the depths of distress and heights of optimism which would test my ability to survive. Many of my adventures in this book fill me with shame. My path is full of missteps, awful choices, uncanny luck, and wild expectations.

In my story, you might glimpse the surprising and strange choices you might have made, had you lived a life like mine.

Chapter 1:
The Red-Eyed Rat

We had really pulled a burglary, a jewel heist to fund a scheme to purchase drugs. Where did we get the guts to do it? Was it guts or bravado? And did we really expect to get away with it?

So here I was. Football star, athlete, Mr. Popular, and a jailbird. A disgrace, a drug dealer, a thief, a convicted felon in a foreign country. What would my family say? And my dear Grandma—how could I ever look her in the eyes again?

I had been riding shotgun with my friend, Weenie, disembarking from the ferry in Algeciras, when the policeman went through the rental car and discovered the hundred kilos of hashish in our duffel bags. Everybody came around and congratulated him like he'd won the lottery, cheering him like a soccer hero.

They handcuffed me and Weenie, drove us to a prison that must have been hundreds of years old, and threw us roughly into a filthy cell. The windows were approximately ten feet up, and the light stayed on high up in the cell. The building could have been there during the Inquisition. But now, Francisco Franco's men were the inquisitors. "Remember the Phalange!"

They let us have our sunglasses, our jeans, our sandals. They took all identification, of course, but not our *dinero*, or our belts. They didn't care if we hung ourselves. I sat with my back against the cell with my other cellmate; the shock made it impossible to speak.

Three days went by, with gruel, beans, and rice, wriggling with little living things: "*Papillon* sauce." I wasn't hungry enough, even on the third day, to try to eat it. They brought us a razor and told us to shave. I didn't really know what was happening. But I thought of burning stakes, Joan of Arc, the Inquisition, or a firing squad. We shaved with cold water and no soap, and since the blades had probably been used thirty times, we just got a little of the stubble off. My hair was already full of lice.

They marched us out single-file, handcuffed from the rear, to an ornate courtroom, where three plump men in their fifties sat, wearing dirty black robes. They assigned a public defender to help us, who spoke broken English, making it difficult to follow the proceedings. They started reading a criminal charges document to us. It sounded like the *Declaration of Death*. This went on for an unbearably long time.

They asked Weenie and me to explain what had happened. Of course we had a pre-arranged story ready, just in case. But when it was my turn, the words came out of my mouth, but I'm not sure what I said. My voice cracked, and tears welled up in my eyes. I tried to regain my composure.

Would they believe us? They had to. We were Americans on a holiday in Spain. We wouldn't rob each other. It had to be the gypsies. When they couldn't solve a crime, it was always the gypsies.

The three judges talked back and forth. The police officer got up on the stand. He seemed to have a new uniform and a shiny new watch, and the spectators cheered him, of course. There seemed to be a few more witnesses, but I had no idea what was going on. They told us to stand, and the middle one banged the gavel. "*Convicto!*" There was a pause, and then the translator spoke. "You will serve six years and a day as a guest of General Franco in his hotel." That was the dream from which I couldn't awaken.

When you have a nightmare, you wake up, and everything is okay. But when you have that nightmare and you try to wake up and you *are* awake, that's the end.

It seemed like a delusion, and it came so fast that it was almost as if I had dreamt it. I felt that it wasn't me there—it was somebody else, and I was looking down on the whole situation in disbelief. Like words in the pages of *White-Jacket*, about the voyages that transformed Melville from a boy into a man. But my own transformation would be a long time coming.

Weenie and I went back to our cells and started a hunger strike and an all-around commotion. It didn't work. A guard in a green jumpsuit came with a billy club, started banging the front of our cell, cursing at us, and decided that we needed to be separated.

Four or five days later, it was time for showers. We were getting ripe. We were lead into the shower room with other sordid prisoners—Arabs, Basques, Spaniards. We were the only Americans. The shower was ice-cold, the towel more like a handkerchief, and the soap stank. Weenie and I decided to protect each other's backs.

One large Moroccan guy was watching us very carefully. I pretended I didn't see him. He was obviously aroused, his member swollen. I was sitting on a stool drying myself when he made an aggressive move towards me. I don't know what happened, but the stool hit the middle of his head, and it split open. There was screaming, there was blood, there were whistles, and we were brought back to solitary. I could tell by the looks of the other inmates that I'd made my point. I had established our alpha position, and I wasn't about to be pursued or intimidated by the "pack."

I was so angry at them and at myself, I felt like smashing him again. I looked around for the next customer. There's always a next customer—when you're looking.

I had a piece of wood with a smelly mattress on it—if you can call it that, a quarter-inch thick, half a pillow, a tin dish for food, and a hole for a toilet.

Unfortunately, I had roommates. The four-footed variety. Weenie and I were in the same cell for the first few days, then we were separated. But Rudy the red-eyed rat and his friends found me. It was war. And I only had my thongs. At first, they were standoffish. Circling, making noises in the middle of the night, bothering my sleep. Then Rudy started making aggressive moves for my toes. He was good-sized—like a cat. Ugly yellow teeth, red eyes, mange. If I had had some bread or something else, any morsel I could spare, I would have fed him and tried to win him over, but I didn't have that luxury. The other problem was the mosquitoes, the relentless mosquitoes biting me non-stop, as my blanket was too small to wrap myself in.

And if that weren't enough, the food—I can't even speak of the food, if you could call it that. And I knew it was only the beginning.

I sat there in the darkness, asking, "What did I do to deserve this?" I knew I couldn't last six years. Impossible. I figured I'd go mad within a year.

With our money, which they hadn't taken, much to our surprise, we were able to buy Carnation milk, cigarettes, delicious Hershey bars, and Valencia oranges.

Things got better, but I kept hearing fireworks, or shots in the street, and a lot of screaming and noise late at night from another part of the prison.

One day, after a couple of weeks, they brought in other inmates who looked like they'd been beaten and kicked. It appeared they needed solitary more than we did, so they put us back in our original cell.

We were able to get writing paper and envelopes and started our campaign to free ourselves. We wrote to everybody we could think of to spring us. We were charged an exorbitant fee for stamps, and, years later, I learned that the letters were never mailed because no one received them.

The only things we had to read were several pamphlets from Tim Leary's lectures and a stained *National Geographic* that I was learning to read upside-down, so it seemed different.

Lighting a cigarette. Waiting for more rats, and the mosquitoes. I ended up soaking cigarettes in water, dipping rags in the liquefied tobacco and wiping it all over myself—my neck, my face, and all my other exposed parts—and the nicotine would stop the mosquitoes from biting. It gave me something to do, a little project every evening. I was looking at nothing, and nothing to do, for six years.

•◊•◊•

As I lay in my cell, cold and hungry, I recalled a sunny afternoon in Long Beach in 1956, when I was working in a Safeway supermarket with my old friend, Mark Newman. We were fifteen, and we were putting food on the shelves to make "hot dog money" in the summer. I think we came up short. We ate more than we shelved. Another friend came into the Safeway market, and told me that somebody from a lower grade had called a girl I liked a "whore" and a "rag." I sent word back that this was not acceptable, and I might have to crush his face if I saw him. The reply came: Meet on the beach at sunset at the end of the Boardwalk with my gang, and they would bring their gang. I talked this over with Newman and we decided to put small kitchen knives in our socks. I had read too many Harold Robbins books.

I was evaluating the situation. The kid I was supposed to meet was a grade under me, but he was six-four, two hundred pounds. Elvis haircut, engineer boots, menacing arms from weightlifting. I myself was six feet, one hundred forty-five. We walked down to the beach, and before we were supposed to have the fight, we were surrounded by our gangs. Mike Kosella, one of the guys from the luncheonette at the Franklin Hotel, who later went over a cliff in a motorcycle and burned in the air at age twenty-two, was with me. They showed up with ten assorted hoods. I didn't like my prospects. We decided to arm wrestle first, which was ridiculous, since his arm was twice the size of mine. But since I had been in football training that summer, he could not move my arm from its position. We pulled and tugged for fifteen minutes. Nothing happened. This was a sort of 1950s warfare.

We backed off. He took his black jacket off, combed his hair like Elvis, smirked, and put a cigarette in his mouth. We all turned to go to the beach. Big mistake on his part. Don't ever turn your back in combat. We walked onto the beach. I was wearing khakis, a T-shirt, and sneakers. We got about twenty feet into the beach when Mike Kosella handed me a "jaw teaser," which is a piece of lead pipe wrapped with adhesive. It felt very comfortable in my hands. I knew if I hit him hard enough he would go down. The red mask came on me, my "ultimate rage"—the blood pulsed through my head, and I was on him, a panther on an ox. He gave up; I used a wrestling hold called the "Princeton," where I was able to put both my hands behind his hands when he reached up to grab my head, and he couldn't move. I don't know if I hit him five or ten times, but the top of his head started to get mushy. He lay motionless for a time, and then he started to move again. We ran.

The next day the rumors were flying around town. Evidently he went to the emergency room and got quite a few stitches.

My mother was very good to me, very supportive, and played the he-can-do-no-wrong card with the police, keeping me out of trouble. "He's just young and learning..." The cops didn't really believe it, but *all right, so he busted the guy's head open,* they didn't really care. My brother was proud of me, even though the guy I smashed was the toughest guy in my brother's class.

The most famous beach club was *El Patio*, which the movie *The Flamingo Kid* was based on. The movie was about us. The good-looking card-playing guy who beat the old man was Harvey Sheldon, a.k.a. Rodney Sheldon. The parking lot attendant in the movie was Jimmy Pullis, who later owned the club "Tracks" in New York City, the hangout for rock 'n' roll musicians. These beach clubs provided great jobs for young guys. I worked at *El Patio* for three summers during high school. We were cabana boys. "Cabana boy, get me ice water." "Cabana boy, I need a club sandwich and a strudel." "Hurry, cabana boy." The tips were good, and their daughters were available.

The clubs brought in name entertainment on the weekends from Tito Puente to Bobby Darin. *El Patio* hosted the great *garmentos*. They lived in huge houses on the swamplands, had spoiled daughters with gold chains, huge bar mitzvahs, long cigars, and polished nails from 1407 Broadway. There were pick-up bars, like Lou's, and Furies, near the railroad tracks in Cedarhurst. That's where all the rich Jews were. I wished I was there again, right now.

•◇•◇•

The battle with the rats continued. Underneath my bed I found a few old logs and pieces of wood and waited for the right opportunity to kill Mr. Red-Eyes, pretending I was asleep. The first few times I missed—he was too fast. Finally, I was able to get a rebound shot and cracked him on the nose, and he disappeared, never to be seen again. After that, the friends he left behind were a piece of cake—they were easy to scare. So all I had to do was deal with the mosquitoes, and, since it was getting colder, they were disappearing. Perhaps, now, I could regain what little sanity I had left.

They started to let us go out into the exercise yard, and I met Felipe. He had been there for ten years. They'd caught him with explosives trying to blow up a police station. One of his hands was blown off, and he had a stump. His English was quite good, and he told me that his family had owned a restaurant in the North of Spain, the Basque area, and after the war they took his dad away, his mother, all his property, and all their animals. He would be getting out in a year.

The next day, it rained terribly—and it rained and it rained and the water came into the cell. It was starting to get dark. I lit another lousy Spanish cigarette, closed my eyes, and thought of college. My memories were my only door to sanity.

•◊•◊•

I was a freshman at Boston University in 1958. My parents let me off at Miles Standish Hall, where my suite was up on the sixth floor. I had a horrible bed with hanging springs, a lumpy mattress, and I kept complaining to the dorm monitor, day after day, the first week, until I could take it no longer.

The red mask came down on me, my eyes pounding, and I don't know what happened, but the entire box-spring, bed, and mattress went out the window into the courtyard, and I was immediately put on probation. I didn't care; I snuck out the following night. I met a family friend who was at another college, and we drove down Commonwealth Avenue to a mixer at one of the women's colleges. His convertible had New York plates. We were driving along, minding our own business, when we got cut off by two huge gorillas with a Boston College sticker on their car. They screamed curses, something like, "Jew pussy, go to the ovens!" or "Death to you all!" and I answered, "Come on back, and we'll see who's the pussies!"

They stopped their car, they got out, and they got out, and they got out. They were big—they must have been the two starting tackles on the B.C. football team. The red mask came on me again; I charged one of them, and my "new friend" ran off screaming, "Don't hurt me! I just had new braces put in!" This happened right in front of the school mixer. Everyone came pouring down from the stairs. I just made it under the car to protect myself, hiding, because they were kicking me and trying to turn the car over. A guy I knew, who later became a good friend, a frat brother from Long Island, the size of one of the football players, took them on. Fortunately, for me, he had been a high school champion heavyweight wrestler. In later years, he would leap out of a thirty-five story office building in Manhattan and kill himself—he was bipolar. But now, he threw one of the gorillas over one of the garbage cans. It appeared he had a red mask, too, because he ripped off their antenna and proceeded to slash the guy who was left. Then he pulled me out from under the car and helped me to the school infirmary. I needed some iodine and bandages. I looked like I'd made a bad bet and lost, but word went around campus quickly, as these things do. The next day everyone wanted me to pledge to their fraternity. I was the Jewish hero.

After the incident, one of the fraternity brothers named Sandy Gallen patted me on the back and said, "Way to go!" I remembered his name years later when I heard he'd become Dolly Parton's partner and Michael Jackson's rep.

After college, I lived at 1012 Lexington Avenue, between 72nd and 73rd on Lexington. I had a one-bedroom apartment for forty-nine dollars a month, a third floor walk-up with French windows. I had a mattress on the floor, some built-in shelves, a bathroom with a bamboo curtain door, a hot plate, and a refrigerator.

•◊•◊•

I could tell through the windows in my prison cell that the sun was out. It must have been a beautiful day. And it must have been Sunday, because I heard singing from the church across from the prison. I broke my last cigarette in half and searched for more memories to keep my spirits up.

I thought about another sunny afternoon, when I was in Long Beach on one of the canals. I was only fifteen. In front of my girlfriend's house was a fifteen-foot boat with an outboard motor. I was with Mark Newman and Joey Burrel, a swimming champ from one of the tough high schools in New York. I'd fought Joey too, but we'd become friends after that. It was warm, and we wanted to go fishing and swimming. We got into a boat which was not ours. Joey, being a pro at stealing cars, got the engine started. We both jumped in and went down the canals out to Reynolds Channel. We were having a good old time, just going around. We knew where everybody would be later in the afternoon—the tennis courts. As the then-popular disc-jockey "Murray the K" would say on his "swinging soirée," it was where we would go with our dates to watch the "submarine races."

As I mentioned, Joey Burrel was a world-class swimmer, and I was pretty good, too. Newman, who came originally from the Bronx, told us he wasn't much of a water man. We started to show off. Everybody was cheering from the shore; they knew who we were. We were doing figure eights, going backwards and forward in circles. We were having a terrific afternoon together, until...

We noticed from going around in all these erratic directions that the back of the boat was filling, and filling quickly. What do you do? Man overboard! Joey went in like a fish, and I was next. It was approximately a half mile to shore, maybe less. No big deal, we were on our way to shore anyway. Newman went down with the ship. He had on big heavy dungarees. Joey was on shore first, already smoking a cigarette. I was coming up second. Of course the boat was sinking, and Newman was struggling out there. His head was underwater. Joey was taking bets, with cigarettes, as to whether Newman would make it.

He came up, he went down, he came up, he went down. Finally, he was able to get up out of the gunk and clumsily started for shore. We had to jump in and swim back out to help him. He was panting and flopping like a wet flounder.

Two days later, my parents woke me at three in the afternoon. There were two detectives who wanted to know what I knew about the boat. They took me down to the police station, put the hot light on, and started questioning me. I didn't crack under the pressure. I never gave up Joey, who was on probation. Newman they already knew about.

So much for my summer of loafing. They told me that I had to pay the man back for his boat, so I got a job sanding cabinets for the entire summer. Everything I made had to be paid back to the boat's owners. Newman had to do the same.

My reminiscing ended when a blood-curdling scream came out of one of the cells. I stuffed rags in my ears. It was a death cry—one of many.

•◇•◇•

Three months into my incarceration, my teeth were bleeding from the diet, and my clothes were all starting to fall apart. I sat down, and was very quiet.

I concentrated, and said very softly, "If I can get out of here, I will change."

I was not religious. I'd been bar-mitzvahed, but after that, or even before, I hadn't given much thought to any God or divine being helping me, but at this point I had nowhere else to go. I decided to try to make a deal. I gave God my word that I would change if I could get out of there, that I would help other people. That I would try to live a moral vision of some kind.

It was getting dark.

I said, "Please get me out of here. I can't take it. Please!"

In the depths of my despair, a powerful fantasy took shape. I imagined a sort of prison Olympics, and I got the guards to go along. It was easy because they would give us extra time to do things if we'd stay out there and be productive—by cleaning up and working on the grounds. So by building the high jump and broad jump pads, I was also able to clean up the grounds. Then I got wood from the woodshop and we made hurdles. And I got them to provide lime so we could make lines on the track, and I set up coaching classes to teach them what I knew. The prison was divided into three parts, and word got out about what we were doing in our part. And others volunteered to do it as well. The guards got involved. Watching us all train made their jobs easier. Most of the inmates were uncoordinated, and many were inept. But they tried; they were good sports. I gave them encouragement and set up competitions—the fifty-yard dash, the high jump—everybody got involved.

One afternoon, there was a commotion, and we discovered that the supervisor of prisons for the southern district of Spain had come by and watched what we were doing. They called me in the office the next day and told me it would be okay to have the games in two weeks, on a Sunday, so the guards could bring their families and have wine and cheese. And then they asked if some of the guards could participate in some events. Why not? It was turning into a carnival, like a baby Olympics!

On the day of the jailhouse Olympics, the stands were packed and there were bands playing loud music, and people were taking pictures. I was planning to pole-vault my way to freedom, but I couldn't isolate myself to take a run at the wall. It was impossible. Everybody was watching me. I got down on my knees, asking, "What am I going to do?"

The next morning, I had a very high fever and diarrhea. I suppose the dream was part of the delirium of being sick.

Suddenly, the main guard banged on my cell, shook the doors and screamed, "¡Andale!"

They chained me and handcuffed me, and put a manacle around my waist and legs, and marched me into the warden's office. They had a conversation, but all I got out of it was, "... *mucho urgente... no más... malo... americanos...*" No good. I didn't know what was going on.

I did not have control over my bowels, and they wouldn't let me go to the *baño*. Instead, they took me to another room, where I saw my suitcase and Weenie's. I had money stashed in my suitcase, and an extra set of keys for the Peugeot that was who knows where. I was sure I was hallucinating as they told me to strip, threw me a towel, and led me into the showers and told me to clean myself up.

I got into my old street clothes, which no longer fit, grabbed my suitcase and Weenie's, and was escorted out through the giant gates. A beat-up bus pulled up with a group of shackled prisoners—men with head and leg wounds, battered and torn— some Basques who had blown up a bank. Perhaps they needed my hotel room. But what about Weenie?

Much to my surprise, the guards escorted me back to the Peugeot to get my personal things. It was still locked up in its own little car prison in customs with hundreds of others. I took out my extra suitcase, a canteen, my walking boots, and some pesetas. I also took the rest of the jewels, gold, and cash I had hidden in the air conditioning system. Luckily, the guards weren't watching me.

Then I got a cab to take me to the Hotel Christina.

I was free. But not Weenie. By sheer luck they had kicked me out to make space for the Basque bombers. But my friend, the guy who came to Europe to help *me* find the love of my life, sat rotting in this hell hole. I had to get him out—somehow. And then I had to find my girl.

Chapter 2:

Francesca

When I first met Francesca, I was working on 34th Street for a children's wear company called Wonder Knit. I called it Wondershit. It was a horrible job, in a horrible building, in the middle of the garment center. They gave me samples, and I called on people and tried to get orders. It was a waste of time. They gave me dead leads, and I was low man on the totem pole.

Before that—before I went in the Army—I worked at Manhattan Shirt Company as an executive trainee in the Time-Life Building. That was fun. Great secretaries, lots of good-looking clothes. I had to wear a hat—menswear—and the building was brand new and stylish.

That's when I first met Muhammad Ali, standing in front of the Americana Hotel, screaming that he was the greatest. We spent an evening together. He was crazy, crazy like a fox. Over the years, I met him several times. Once in Miami, at the Coconut Grove, while I was on the lam. He was training for the Sonny Liston fight at the 5th Street Gym. I went there to watch him train and scream at him, and he screamed back, "I'm the greatest!" Then I'd go watch Sonny Liston work out. He looked like a killer, which he was. He looked like he was going to rip Ali's head off, but, in the championship fight, Ali won with a TKO.

Many years later, I met Ali at a private party at Xenon's, the number two club after Studio 54, when he was with his wife, Victoria. He was out of boxing by then, and sadly, in the first stage of Parkinson's. But he was magnificent, and is still one of our greatest champions—a testimony to a fighting spirit, inspiring and uplifting.

Back to Wondershit: At ten o'clock, I would go to Grant's on 42nd Street, have a couple of hot dogs and go to the movies. I came out at lunchtime, blinking in the sunshine. I went for a steak at Tad's for a dollar twenty-nine, and then back to the movies. At four-thirty, I came back to the office, with my shirt open and my tie hanging, and told my boss about all the people I'd seen. I had copied their names from building directories. I got petty cash for lunch, and the sales manager grilled me. I chewed mints to hide the smell of onions on the hot dogs.

Then I'd start over, wearing my suit and tie. I looked forward to coming home, putting on a costume, smoking a big joint, and walking my skunk.

I first met Francesca on a Sunday afternoon in the spring of 1963.

A friend had been invited to a party on 5th Avenue by the famous designer Oleg Cassini, and he asked me to join him. I surveyed the room in my usual way, the predator pursuing game. It was not a typical New York party, but a cocktail party for aristocrats. Everyone was well dressed in an intimidating array of designer clothes, and a pianist played softly. As I looked around the room, I saw a young woman in a white Chanel suit, looking very proper. I eased my way over and asked her if I could get her a drink.

"Yes."

When I returned, I said, "I'm Barry. Do you mind if I visit with you?"

"My name is Francesca," she said. "Why don't you sit down?"

I had never met a Francesca. We sat down and got acquainted. She was about five-ten, well proportioned, and my age—twenty-two—with brown hair, light eyes, nice pearls, and a crested ring. Our conversation was full of playful putdowns—on her part. She asked me what I did, and I told her I was a student at Boston University.

"Oh, not Harvard?"

"No," I said. "I'm not a Harvard boy."

I learned later that her father had donated a wing to Harvard, the Spaulding Wing. She asked me if I'd ever been to Rome or Paris.

"No…"

She asked me where I was from.

"Long Island."

"From the Hamptons?"

"No, I'm from Long Beach."

"Oh. I don't quite know where that is."

"Well, it's near Jones Beach…"

"Oh," she said. "Is that near the Hamptons?"

It became clear that all she knew was the Hamptons. I had the impression that she wanted to know if I was Jewish, but she was not asking.

A friend of hers came over and spoke with her in French. Later she switched to Italian with someone else. I was sure it was all to impress me, and it did.

It was mutual attraction. She was clearly very bright, and not an American. She was born in Geneva during the war, grew up there and in Rome, and was then sent to a fine women's school in the States. She spoke with a slight European accent—or at least she was trying to, even though, as I found out later, she spoke perfect English. She was just having some fun with me. I was out of my element, and she knew it. She was flirting with me and trying to be fetching. Still, I was impressed. She told me she'd just gotten back from Rome, where she worked part time, and then we realized that we both knew Tim Leary, whose LSD experiments I'd participated in at Cambridge. She used every chance to name-drop. I found it amusing. Well, we clicked, and after a few more drinks, she gave me her address on 64th and Park. She told me that if I'd like to, I might call on her. I said I'd like to. She gave me her card. Her last name was long, hyphenated, aristocratic, and unreadable to a dyslexic.

The next day, I called her up, and she said, "Why don't you come by? We'll have a drink." Her place wasn't far from my apartment. It was in an imposing, block-long building. After the doorman rang up and showed me to the elevator, the elevator man took me up. She and her mother had an entire floor on Park Avenue.

I had an apartment with a skunk when I first met Francesca. I'd just broken up with a beautiful blonde model who was very angry with me, for good reason. I came home after work one day and found only her neutered skunk. I called him Treesqueak. He enjoyed my house and me, since we were both nocturnal. He didn't sleep much. Give him a little cheese, some pastrami on rye with a pickle, and he was happy—a happy skunk. On a nice Saturday, I took Treesqueak under my arm, walked over to 72nd and Park, put his leash on, and walked up the avenue. I had my safari hat on. I met lots of women and got plenty of phone numbers. Treesqueak was a chick magnet.

The lights in my apartment were all fluorescent. It looked like a crash pad. You tripped going in the front door, and landed on the mattresses, and then the skunk would nip your ankles. It was a trap. I remember several dates I had that I reconsidered. When Treesqueak raised his butt and stomped, they wound up fleeing down the stairs. He couldn't do anything, but that was his sign to get out of my place.

The first time Francesca came to my apartment, I was intimidated. But she had lived at 103 MacDougal Street, so she'd had her share of Greenwich Village. She babysat for Mary Travers of the singing trio Peter, Paul and Mary. She had been a hippie, too—a hippie countess. It appeared my skunk and my apartment and my attitude worked. She thought I was "different." I was. I'd say, "Don't speak English. I don't want to know what you're saying." I liked her to speak to me in French and Italian.

Francesca and I started to hang out on the street at night—mainly near MacDougal and Bleeker Street, and Washington Square. I found it very annoying that at parties, she and her friends would speak French and Italian. I didn't know what they were talking about, and they looked at me like either I wasn't there, or "My God, he doesn't even speak French! He doesn't know Italian!" I went out and got a couple of phrasebooks, but it didn't help. They spoke so quickly that it went right over my head, but sometimes I could figure out part of it—a lot of it was restaurant French. But when they bent their elbows and leaned forward over a demitasse, I couldn't understand, but I acted like I did, nodding, bobbing, and weaving. I didn't like it, though, so I tried to have more one-on-one dates. But when we went to the discotheques, everybody was so loud it really didn't matter.

She gravitated to the village, Bohemian-type restaurants and coffeehouses, and that was fine with me. Since I'd lived in Beacon Hill in the Bohemian section of Back Bay, I got along very well with—as we called them—beatniks. The restaurants and clubs in those days all had that French sound.

We sat in the old Fillmore, watching a new group playing "My Evil Ways." They were called Santana, and everyone cheered. Afterwards, we'd go down to the Hip Bagel, have a one o'clock dinner, and watch the beatniks and the hippies come in and out. On MacDougal Street, you'd see a man in a dress rollerskating down the middle of the street throwing rose petals and singing at the top of his lungs. And on the corner this weird guy with a paunch played the ukulele with his girlfriend, Tinkerbell, and he called himself Tiny Tim. He had long, long hair, an ugly beak, and an irritating, high voice.

Everything was tie-dye, colors, beads, peace signs, exposed breasts, people hugging each other, and Hari Krishnas singing in Central Park, with marijuana smoke wafting through the air. Everyone had a joint, and every Saturday and Sunday there was a happening. The Sheep Meadow was full of freaks. Turn on and drop out. People would go to relieve themselves behind trees and never return to where they started from. They could end up in California or Florida with another group. It didn't matter, it really didn't. Somebody would sit down on your blanket, and they would think that's where they started from. And you'd just nod your head and say, "Dig it, man. Dig it."

It was easy to get lost.

•◊•◊•

Francesca had taught me about pharmaceuticals. I didn't know a Secanol from a baseball when I met her.

She lived on MacDougal Street, and was living, or hanging out with, amphetamine addicts. She previously had a boyfriend who hit her when she took his drugs away from him and he was jonesing.

She took Dexamyl to lose weight. She loved it.

One interesting part of my relationship with Francesca was meeting all her friends. They were so unlike the people I grew up with. They were bilingual and trilingual, well-traveled, and extensively educated. There were also musicians, hookers, club owners, magicians, and chess players. We did have something in common, though, because I had a group of friends that were Beacon Hill Beats, coming down from Beacon Street to the Back Bay Area. I lived in Beacon Hill when I was going to college—B.U. and Emerson—and her family was from Boston, but a different side of the tracks. Their set owned the industrial complex of our country, our manufacturing, and our banking. For example, she was friends with Richie and Brigitte Berlin, who were in Andy Warhol's movies. Brigitte's father was the chairman of the board of the *New York Herald Tribune.*

The streets I walked down were where her ancestors settled after Plymouth Rock, Back Bay. I would sit and study in the library at Harvard, where her great-grandfather had a building named after him. They all got off the boat early and had a good head-start. Years later, when I came up to Boston with her to see her doctors and her trust fund lawyer, it was strange for me to learn that her allowance came from money earned three or four hundred years ago, managed by the bluebloods on State Street. Her mother told me they'd had a house in Pride's Crossing, with a hundred gardeners and servants. When I saw a photograph of the place, I understood why they needed so many gardeners. They had had two boats during World War II. FDR had asked them to turn them into hospital ships. There was a house in Saint Thomas, an apartment in Paris, another in Cannes, villas in Rome and Spoleto, an apartment on Park Avenue, and an island, Upper St. Regis, in the Adirondacks. It was on three hundred acres, with an original "shabby chic" 1920s fishing lodge and about fifteen small cabins. Of course, it had a boat house, a pool house, a recreation room, a lot of dead animal heads hanging on walls, and Adirondack furniture. The only way you could get there was by boat or seaplane. Everyone they knew owned Criss-Crafts and GarWoods, and they had sailboats, which they called "items" and "oh-boats." The big ones were the items and the small ones were the oh-boats. Around the island, they had camps where the Pratts, the Whitneys, the Posts, and other robber barons lived.

I don't really remember my first meeting with her mother. I just remember she was in the back room, rolling around on the floor, cutting her ankles on booze bottles. Or she would call long distance from Sierra Leone or the Spoleto Festival. The conversations never made Francesca particularly happy, and later, after meeting the Contessa, I could understand why. She had nothing good to say about anyone, particularly me.

Francesca did not love her mother. It was all about the money, because nobody could love this woman. She weighed two-hundred fifty pounds in a muumuu, had a Marlon Brando haircut, and could pass for Orson Welles. No longer did she look like a debutante from Boston who'd married the handsome young Italian Count. She looked like a bag lady with a leatherette pocketbook full of hundreds. And most of the time, she smelled like she could use a good bath. Everybody called her "Moomie"— "our sweet Moomie"—and she dispensed hundred-dollar bills like a machine. All the years I knew her, I never saw her have anything other than hundred-dollar bills. I don't think she was allowed to carry tens or twenties, and the hundred dollar bills always came out of a brown envelope from the bank. She threw them around like dirty Kleenex, crushed up. She had a very high voice, like Francesca's. And, of course, she called everybody "Daaaarling!" And it was always "us" and "them." I was a "them."

These were weird times for me. I was working at Wonder Knit, my pregnant girlfriend had had an abortion and left me, and I'd just met Francesca, a countess. I also had to go to National Guard meetings out in Long Island, since I was still in the Army Reserves. Besides this, I had met Eve, who was entering law school at NYU, and wanted to know if I knew anybody who would pay for her services. She was a hooker in training and wanted to know if I knew anything about it. Jerry Cole, my former Emerson schoolmate, was now trying to hustle business for a young girl so he could support his habit. I asked him if he could let me borrow his "trick book" because I had a rookie who wanted to learn the business.

Then Kennedy was killed. My reserve unit called me from Hempstead, Long Island and told me to come down and pick up live ammunition. We might be going to war. I didn't do wars.

Two nights later, amid national shock, and after they buried Kennedy at Arlington, I was down in the Village with Francesca, a hooker friend of hers, and Lenny Bruce, whom I had met through Francesca. Lenny was getting ready to do a show at the Fillmore. He was warned to keep it low-key because of President Kennedy's death. That night Lenny gave a passionate rap for two hours. It was about the "big conspiracy." He was staying at a skanky hotel on 8th Street, and he died of a drug overdose soon after that.

Later I visited the grassy knoll and thought about what Lenny had said. He kept telling the truth, even though they kept trying to shut him up. Years later, his mother told me about how Lenny kept getting harassed. The police would break up his shows because he was considered a subversive.

A week later, the sales manager called me in for a meeting and told me that they were cutting back because of poor business. Last in, first out. I gave him his samples back. Bunched in with them were some dirty shirts, hot dog wrappers, and movie tickets. It was time for unemployment, and I signed up. I needed money to feed Treesqueak and take Francesca to dinner.

That was the last time I ever worked for anybody but myself. I swore that from then on I would never have an employer, and I've been very fortunate since then. I looked at my options; I could be a pimp or I could be a count. My life was wide open. It was time to channel my insanity. Some friends offered me a position, but it was not exactly what I was looking for. They wanted to know if I could get acid, pot, or anything else for "certain people" and their friends. What should I do? Be illegal? Deal drugs? Prostitution?

I had no overhead, a skunk to feed, a fifty-dollar rent-controlled apartment, and unemployment. I hung out in the Village, watching chess, drinking coffee in the shops, listening to jazz, feigning to everybody that I was looking for a job. I didn't do well as a man of the day. It was time to be a man of the night.

Francesca had a small trust fund, but it was enough to go out for intimate dinners and to clubs with music—general hanging-out money. Plus I had my unemployment, which was around seventy dollars a week. We were doing fine, and I was getting to meet her girlfriends and her family, going to parties, and becoming a disco aficionado; I liked Le Club, Doubles, and Hippopotamus.

A friend of mine, Lukie from California, came by with some California grass and made a score. He suggested that we all go down to Florida for the sun. So Weenie went to Florida with Lukie and some friends, and Francesca and I followed in a rented car. We drove straight through.

We checked in at a hangout in Coconut Grove. We went to the racetrack, to the beach, hung out, and had a good time eating stone crabs at Joe's. At the dog track, we ran out of money, but we put a few of our last ten-dollar bills down on a dog. That old greyhound with its crooked leg won. It paid about fifty bucks, so we had a bunch of money. My next recollection was of opening my eyes in the middle of the night, looking at the speedometer on the brand-new XKE we rented to drive back to New York. It was at 120 mph, and Francesca was driving. The only problem was we were going through a gas station. I was terrified—I screamed, she slowed down, and I took the wheel. Our practice honeymoon was over, and we were heading back to pills and needles.

We got back to the city and were invited to a party at Albert Grossman's house on Bedford Street. He managed Peter, Paul, and Mary, the Birds, and Bob Dylan. Francesca was friendly with Paul Stookey, and Peter Yarrow, who were all at the party. Grossman was one of the most powerful managers in the music business, and we all had a great evening, sitting around, listening to stories about groups about to happen, groups that missed, and how hard it was to make it. He was a charming, thoughtful host.

Francesca's mother, the Contessa, was terribly upset about our relationship. It wasn't proper, she said, and decided that the best thing to make the relationship go away was a sea voyage. This was the wealthy person's traditional method of discouraging relationships that were considered undesirable.

One of Francesca's girlfriends told me that she was leaving that day for Europe. I went down to the docks to the *Leonardo da Vinci*, and there she was in her cabin suite with a few friends. Fortunately, the Contessa was nowhere in sight. Francesca hadn't had the guts to tell me what she was up to and looked quite surprised to see me there.

"What are you doing?" I asked.

She was flustered. "I think it's best if I go to Europe and give you a chance to think. You know, I'll take an ocean voyage, and we'll think about it."

"What's to think about?" I asked. "You're going on an ocean voyage because you're afraid you're going to lose your allowance. It doesn't make any sense. Just don't go."

"Well, my mother bought the ticket. It's thousands of dollars, it's all set up, and I've got to."

I understood. She didn't want to go, but she had to go. In those families it's all about the money. And the attitude of the parents is that you're not a real adult, you're not responsible, you don't get your allowance, and I'll tell you what to do.

"Well," I said, "I'm going to go find you if you leave."

"We'll see about that."

"I'll be coming after you," I insisted.

They blew the whistle. Everybody who was going to go with her was on board.

We embraced.

"I'll see you in Roma," I said.

"We'll see," she said again.

I came ashore, and the boat left.

Chapter 3:

Abroad with Weenie and Fritzie

It didn't take long before I decided I had to get Francesca back. I told Weenie I was going to Europe with Fritzie to get the woman who had left me out of fear due to an overbearing mother. So, in the late spring of 1964, Fritzie and I left for London on a TWA flight from JFK. All I had was a one-way ticket, and my parents were not happy.

Weenie met us at in Paris at The Whorehouse Hotel.

•◇•◇•

I first met Weenie in pre-school. He had buck teeth, and even at three and a half, pimples and bad skin. He was smaller than most of the kids, and he always seemed to have a handkerchief attached to his hand.

But Weenie became an acquaintance in high school. He was a year older, so we lived in different worlds, but he was always in the background. I went to Boston U. and he went to C.W. Post and drove a cab to support himself.

While in college he started to look almost human. He seemed more attractive, and his teeth weren't as yellow or prominent. He became friends with my friend, Charlie, and several other guys who hung out at night at the beach. I remember playing football with him at the malls. Subsequently, Weenie went into the commercial real estate business. He was working with Charlie when I had my floating whorehouses going.

Later on, I heard Weenie had bought a house in Topanga Canyon—his sister had given him the money. He also opened one of the first big health food and natural food stores in the country, which became a magnet for celebrities in the '60s. It was the happening place. You could see Warren Beatty, Julie Christie, Charles Bronson, and Charlie Manson (serial killers have to eat, too). And I heard more good things about Weenie. He was getting tan, his hair was growing longer, and he was getting trim—as much as he could, since he had always been quite an eater.

A few years later, way after college, in 1971, I bumped into Weenie, and he asked me to visit him in Topanga Canyon. I went out there, where he had a fifteen-acre spread with a 1940s house on top of it. At this point, he had converted to vegetarianism and become a disciple of Swami Muktananda. He was associated with Ram Dass, as well as various other New Age luminaries. Anyway, I enjoyed his place and my first experience of organic food from his store. While I stayed there, I ate that food for about a week. Though I was constantly in the bathroom, I felt great.

By now Weenie was wearing silk suits and Birkenstock shoes, chasing women obsessively, and scoring. But he also let me know he was ready for a new adventure.

I happened to run into one of my old friends, Fritzie, from Boston—a used car salesman from a well-to-do family who sported diamond rings on every finger. He was ruggedly handsome with dark, curly hair and knew how to get what he wanted, in the spirit of a "bad boy."

I introduced Weenie to Fritzie, and they didn't get along at all—Fritzie with his diamonds and his pointy shoes, Weenie with his Birkenstocks and his checkered handkerchief still hanging from his back pocket, not quite in keeping with his silk suit.

•◊•◊•

My adventure with Fritzie and Weenie started out innocent enough. We were just tourists—but with a mission. I remember the smell of fresh bread, the wonderful coffee and milk, and this delectable pastry with sweet butter and jam. It was difficult to get used to only one bathroom on the floor, since the girls were washing at ten in the morning for their work on the stroll, on the Left Bank.

Weenie showed up at my hotel with a car, a green Peugeot. I wanted to walk, so I declined. An American in Paris, I felt like Gene Kelly and immediately bought a beret. I went to the Algerian section of Paris, a dangerous part of town. I found the drugs there to be pricey, and started to think about supplying the Algerians with some that would be more affordable, yet profitable for us. But how to move the drugs when we had them?

I lived in Technicolor for the first time in my life. I walked and walked until I was in front of the Louvre, went in, and didn't come out until it was dark. The paintings, the sculpture, Leonardo, Michelangelo, a world of art on a level I'd never seen. It was so moving. That night, we all met off the *rue Dragon* in a café, smoked our *Gauloises*, choked, and watched the nightlife. The dress, the women, the gentlemen—all were magnificently colorful. It's not only as if the fabrics were clinging to them— they were painted on. The hats, the matching bags, the stockings with seams—*oh, là-là!*—didn't leave much to the imagination. And the guys, their suits, their style—it was the Pierre Cardin era. Fluffy shirts, Edwardian jackets, and beautiful handmade boots.

Finally, we got to sleep at dawn, and the Egg-Man showed up, screaming about eggs and chickens in his wagon. He drove us crazy. We ran down to buy all his eggs and his chickens to get rid of him so we could sleep. He loved us. There were children running around with croissants, and though the building didn't actually have a lobby, it opened right out into the street. The bathroom walls were peeling, revealing old German newspapers underneath.

That night, we got dressed up and went out to the Place Pigalle to see the can-can dances. I imagined I saw Lautrec sitting at the next table. It was great. The lights, the lighting, the food, the waiters. I didn't want to leave. Finally, they warned us to be careful and to take a cab because the area could be dangerous late at night. Fritzie was missing, of course. He had left with a can-can dancer. Weenie and I shared a cab with two German girls and an English guy. They invited us back to their hotel, which was behind the Eiffel Tower, and we stayed up all night talking about Sartre, art, rock n' roll, and sex. I was so excited to be in Paris, to be entering a world at the center of European culture.

We were planning on leaving in a few days for Italy. They gave me the map, and after I gave directions for a while, we found that we were still in the south of France, and Italy was nowhere in sight. It might have been my dyslexia and drunkenness, or maybe I had subconsciously wanted to avoid Francesca. At any rate, I had taken us in the wrong direction—we were going in circles.

Since Fritzie's uncle's friend had a vineyard in France, we decided to go there. The two girls from London were still with us, and the Peugeot was running like a dream. When we arrived at the vineyard, we were given a warm welcome. We started tasting and tasting. *Fromage* and wines. Reds, whites, purples, Beaujolais...

I called Francesca, and she said she had missed me. I could have gone to see her, but we took off instead toward the temptations of the French Riviera rather than Italy. It was a little town called Juan-les-Pins in Cape Antibes. That's where the first Whisky a Go Go opened, and that was our first stop. Dancing in a corner was Brigitte Bardot. Alain Delon was there, and Sophia Loren, politicians, industrialists, sheiks in pajamas and robes, music blaring away, sports cars pulling up and screeching... I was dazed and confused. And there I was, on the same dance floor with all these people.

The French beach was near the Carlton Hotel. It was nothing like Coney Island or Long Beach. The women walked out on the sand, put their little blankets or straw mats down, oiled their bodies after removing their bikini tops and bottoms. They put bottle caps on their nipples so they didn't get burned—and, as I was at the height of my sexual energy, it was very difficult for me to just sit there. Most of the women, when they got up, at least put their bikini bottoms on, but still went topless for hours. There were strippers from Berlin, stewardesses from Denmark, starlets from Paris, and assorted princesses, counts and countesses, dukes and viscounts, all mingling with the masses. After the sun went down, we walked over to the boat basin, going from one yacht to another. Each was grander than the next.

Gold bathrooms, malachite kitchens, round beds, square beds, upside-down beds, mirrors on the ceilings, caviar, champagne, shrimp cocktail, hashish, acid... There was no end to it. From boat to boat to boat. People in rooms, in lounge chairs, on decks. Many people passed out and then woke to dress in formal attire for the evening at the Palm Casino. Damn! I was James Bond.

I saw one guy at the *chemin de fer* table, baccarat, lose three quarters of a million dollars in two hours. All he did was chain-smoke cigarettes from a gold cigarette holder. No emotion. I heard that he owned some Greek islands and some shipping companies. I spent two months doing this. At the Carlton Hotel, they started to put the banners up for the film festival. After a couple of weeks, I was so jaded that the naked women made no impression on me; the boats all looked the same, and it was actually getting boring. It was like going to Hugh Hefner's house for a twentieth Playboy party. Enough.

•◇•◇•

Algeciras is beautiful. It's right on the Mediterranean, and you can look directly at the Straits of Gibraltar. On a boat across to Tangiers, we came close to those straits, and I heard strange, loud sounds. It looked like an earthquake making the rocks tremble, but it was the monkeys that were moving all over the mountain.

Tangiers is one of the great cities for intrigue, romance, and getting lost. The characters are right out of *Casablanca*, people who lost their identities and lost themselves. I heard French, German, and different Arabic dialects coming from the finest restaurants and dives, with a smattering of English and Spanish.

Jerry Cole, an old doper friend, had a room on the second floor looking out over the city for forty cents a night. It seemed extraordinary to run into him in Tangiers, but then I realized that the drugs were cheap there, and it all made sense. I remember going down to the post office and watching William Burroughs pick up his mail. A lot of other Americans were there: Ginsberg, Gregory Corso, Ferlinghetti (*Coney Island of the Mind*)... and there was a branch of the Fat Black Pussycat Cafe from MacDougal Street.

The days were blazing and the nights were cool. I heard jazz coming out of several buildings, and I met hippies from England and Germany putting together caravans to head for India and go back on the silk route through Pakistan and the Khyber Pass, to find God. Everybody asked you if you wanted to find God.

Fritzie was a big guy, hard and mean. We didn't want to cross him. We didn't know that his jewelry was mixed up with her jewelry. But then again, it was all there to be taken.

Fritzie had met a woman in London who had a lot of money. She was older than the rest of us and not particularly attractive—sort of Hyde Park English and stuck up. She liked to allude to a castle that she had. She rented a villa on the ocean in Torremolinos, and the lunatics moved in, namely Weenie and me, the two girls we had picked up on the way, and another guy who had a professional-looking movie camera. Our plan was to go down to the beach, say we were movie producers from California, and ask people if they'd like to be in our movie. We went down to the beach and found many starlet types, although most didn't speak English. We brought a group back to the villa and asked them to put on some white sheets we'd taken off the beds; then we lit candles and told them it was going to be a very devotional religious film. We bought wine and sangria— everyone walked around half-naked in sheets on the beautiful veranda in a mysterious ceremony that we devised.

Torremolinas was growing popular, as was the Costa Brava. All the nightclubs were outside, the music played on, and they were right along the beach. Unfortunately, the *"Guardia Sevilla"* guarded the beach so nobody would go out and try and do the old in-and-out. They were the keepers of the church and the morality watchers.

The English lady didn't particularly like what we were doing and voiced her opinion. Nobody listened to her for a few days, but she continued to complain. Finally, Weenie told me that we needed to get her to "chill." I pointed out that she had paid the rent and asked him what his plans were.

"I have no plans," he said, "but she has lots of money." Weenie and I had a yelling argument, and then we ended up talking about it. We saw that she had some nice jewels. Perhaps it was time to get out of there, after all. Her Ladyship was going around banging pots and pans, telling everybody to leave and breaking up the party. We figured it wasn't going to last much longer, and it was time to get back on the road.

For several weeks, we had been talking about going down to North Africa because we'd heard about all the action in Tangiers. Even in Paris, people had mentioned that it was a dry period for hashish, and that there was a good opportunity if we wanted to get into the drug trade there. So we decided to get involved in the drug trade in Paris. We would get some drugs and go sell them to the Beatles. Obviously we were delusional, but that was the plan. We figured we could get away with taking Her Ladyship's jewelry. But we'd have to get out of there fast and fence it. In Spain it would be hot, but in Africa we could just weigh out the gold because it's a commodity. Then we could buy huge quantities of hashish.

Fritzie argued with us about leaving. We had told him about Africa, asked him what he was doing with that unpleasant woman, urged him to go into action. But he didn't want to go, so that was that. He wouldn't be in on our heist, and he wouldn't even know about it. Weenie and I decided to set up our alibis the next day. We went to the beach and spent the day making sure we were in full sight of everybody. I pretended I didn't feel well and went back to the villa to sleep. And I had them call a doctor and give me a sedative. I didn't take the pills; I faked it. So I was covered. And Weenie took the car and pretended he was going into town.

I went upstairs and took the jewels—and then some.

Later, when the police came and searched, the doctor testified that I was knocked out cold, couldn't move, and had a high fever. So I couldn't have done it, and, of course, I couldn't have heard anything.

Everybody believed it.

When I had sneaked into Her Ladyship's room and taken her jewelry bag, I was certain that she had more jewelry, even though there was the unexpected windfall of the gold and cash. I buried the bag in a nearby park right away and before everyone came back from the beach, where nobody could find it. We had no idea Fritzie's jewelry was also in the bag.

When everyone got back to the house, there was an uproar. Fritzie and Her Ladyship called the police, and a Spanish Inspector Clouseau showed up with his partner. They interviewed me, Weenie, and the girls, and then they called in the maid and the driver. This went on and on, twenty-four hours of interviewing everyone in the house.

After the police let us go, Weenie and I said goodbye and headed toward Africa. We stopped first in Barcelona and waited until midnight two days later, and then we drove back 200 kilometers to dig the stuff up and take it with us. I remember thinking, *What happens if they picked us up right now? Two Americans, in the middle of the night, with a bunch of gold, jewelry, and cash!*

But we were stupid, and we thought we had big balls, so we kept going.

With the jewelry bag hidden in our car, we rented a second car. We drove into Algeciras and took the boat across the water with both cars. We reached Ceuta, the Spanish port, where we found a car storage place. We paid three months in advance, leaving the bigger car, the Peugeot, there to come back for later. Then we took the smaller car and drove into French Morocco and into the glorious city of Tangiers. The plan was that when we took the boat back, we would have a car stashed away that nobody had seen and was clean, and when we stashed our things in there, nobody would know. We had the jewelry, the gold, and some cash, and we would somehow get a large supply of some of the best drugs in the world and go sell them to the Beatles. What could go wrong?

In Tangiers, we got rooms at a nice hotel, since we had the money. We wanted to be above the hippies in the street and look like college kids with a few bucks.

On our third night in Tangiers, we heard about a guy in the Kasbah who was part American and part Moroccan. The word was he had good shit, and we could do a deal. This was from somebody we met in town, who somebody else told us was pretty reliable. Our guy knew somebody who knew somebody's friend, so we thought *we* knew somebody.

We went into the Kasbah, where if you turn around the wrong way you suddenly don't know where you are. We knocked on a door and met an Arab American with a big smile and a gold tooth. He had some cool John Coltrane jazz going, and we found ten people on big cushions, smoking hashish and drinking Scotch and vodka. Some were shooting up in a corner. It was an opium den—without opium. Finally, we worked our way in and met a man we called Hajji, since he had been to Mecca. We talked with him until late in the night. We tried everything, and bounced off the walls like kangaroos. We were gone.

We went into the bedroom where Hajji had a triple beam scale, and told him we had some goods. We showed him some of the gold, and he weighed it out. After talking to him at length, we figured his information was good, but we didn't want to do any business with him.

At two or three in the morning, the guests began to drift out. Hajji kept looking at us and talking to another guy in the corner. We realized maybe we shouldn't be there in the middle of the night with a pocketful of gold. Suddenly, there was a deafening, bloodcurdling scream, and then a thud. Everybody started screaming, and we all got straight pretty quick. Everybody who was still there started to take off. Weenie and I were right with them, except they all disappeared.

It was a corner apartment on a street that was deeply rutted with ancient stones. I stepped out and became terrified. I could see stars through the top of the Kasbah, but my feet were wet as if it were raining. I looked down. My feet were *red*. There was a big pool of blood.

We could see now that there was a whole pool of blood spreading all over the ground. We ran. A left turn—a right turn—left—right—left—right. Ten minutes later, we were back on the same street. We definitely had a problem. We were stoned; we were lost. And then we heard footsteps coming up behind us, faster and faster.

"Holy shit! They're following us!" We were high, we were paranoid because we were high, we were lost, and we didn't know the way out. We tore off through the Kasbah again. Then I said, "That's the street!" We heard running footsteps pursuing us. We saw some empty old tin garbage cans, and we heaved them against the wall in the direction we were running. We made as much noise as we could, yelling and screaming. Lights started to go on around us. We took our thongs off and sprinted out of the bazaar. Somehow we found our way back to the hotel. Once we got to our rooms, I washed my feet off and threw up.

Someone must have been held up right outside the door of Hajji's place. But whoever was chasing us, they left us alone after that, after we'd made all the noise. We were extremely careful from then on. We began to grow beards and kept a low profile.

We decided to find the right man to take us to the right place for kif, and we were turned on to Ali by someone from the hotel who seemed to know his business. Ali said he'd take us to the mountains where they grew fantastic kif, and he took us for a hairy ride in our Siata.

We ended up in a tiny village. He said, "Okay, now we've got to go up this mountain, where there's a plateau. And they'll be waiting there."

We looked at this mountain we had to climb and realized that we'd been stupid. We were wearing thongs and tank tops. So we took some mescaline, took out the knapsack with our loot and made our way up the mountain. We were young and in shape, but this was crazy. It was scorching, and, after what seemed like hours, we reached the top. We were parched. Our new friend brought us to some man's house; it was a one-story with a flat roof, dirt floors, and old peeling shutters. Tattered weavings hung on the doors, and a steady traffic of goats and chickens wandered in and out. The man didn't speak English, but through an interpreter, he told us that they were going to bring us samples. We could taste them all and choose what we wanted. He offered us a very good price, which made sense, since we were going right to the source.

That night, they killed a chicken and made us couscous. We took a risk and told them we had some of the money with us. And they brought out several samples for us to try and smell. The problem with testing drugs is that once you're high you can't even tell which is A, B, or C, so we did an "Eenie-meenie-minie-mo," and told him we wanted what seemed like the sample with the finest resin and oil.

He said okay.

We gave them a deposit, and were told they would deliver the drugs to us in Tangiers in three weeks. On that particular night we were quite paranoid, and neither of us slept well because of all the sampling. And I must say, killing the chicken for us had definitely made it all quite strange. It's also strange when you can't speak each other's language, but you're stoned, so you speak anyway, and then you get all these imaginary conversations going on.

They brought us pillows, and we survived the night on the mountain. It was actually beautiful where we slept, out on the roof.

The next day we went back down the mountain to our little car, which we were going to have to get rid of soon, and waited three weeks. And then the shit came in. We tested it, and it was dynamite.

We hunted around town and picked up a sailor who needed a lift back. We brought duffel bags with *U.S. NAVY* stenciled on them, wrapped the stuff up in plastic and put it all in the bags. Then we put diving equipment on top and camouflaged it pretty well. We put the bags in the car, drove all the way out of French Morocco back to Ceuta, got the Peugeot out of storage, and transferred the kif into it. We crossed the water again, gave the *dirty* car we'd been using to cross the border to my old junkie friend, Jerry Cole, who was a junkie, and switched to the *clean* car.

We watched customs personnel unloading for two days and timed our approach. We had heard that on Sunday afternoons, customs workers never bothered to open people's trunks; they were typically drunk and inattentive because they would soon be off on the four o'clock boat to spend time with their families, and were anxious to leave. So we timed everything carefully for Sunday afternoon, figuring we would be safe.

Unfortunately, that Sunday they were more attentive than usual. Weenie drove us onto the boat, which took us across the Straits, and then, for some reason, they opened up all the trunks at customs. And we got caught.

Chapter 4:

Going Home Alone

I left Algeciras and checked into the Hotel Christina in Málaga, where I took many showers and kissed the ground. The next morning, I woke up in the hotel and sat on my balcony, sipping my coffee and fresh Valencia orange juice, with *real* eggs and real bacon, nothing powdered. I looked up at the sky and truly felt that something majestic had happened. I was sure that somebody interceded for me at a "higher" level to get me out of prison and put me in this suite, looking out at the blue Mediterranean.

Right then and there, I promised God or Whoever was up there or Whoever was listening—the Universe, the Omnipotent One, an Archangel—Anybody—that I would never again do anything to put myself or my family in jeopardy or shame them, that I would be appreciative, and that I would try to serve. The Spanish judge had spat on my passport because I was American. That had rankled me, and I vowed never again to embarrass my country.

I had the right intention, but I was too young to keep my word. I really meant it at the time. But the stronger I got, and the farther away from Spain, the more I forgot about my promise to God. It took me many years to fulfill that promise. Still, I was filled with a sense of gratitude, and I had a chance in the world again.

My clothes didn't fit, so I took Weenie's. I hadn't realized how much weight I'd lost. I felt a little silly in his colors, but they were clean, and so was I.

I took a third-class train to Madrid to see if I could make contact with someone, or find some way to get Weenie released.

I called my parents. I can't remember much of the conversation, but I remember my shame. There had been something about our heist and capture in the New York newspapers.

I couldn't think of a way to help my friend. I knew that Weenie was getting letters from his parents, so they knew what had happened, but I didn't have the courage to talk to them myself.

It was time to get on the road.

I went to the local haberdashery and bought a bunch of traditional Spanish clothing for my trip. I was still plagued by the remnants of dysentery and extremely paranoid. I took a third class train from Málaga to Madrid—me and the chickens, everybody, and everything else that goes third-class. I checked into a fleabag hotel in Madrid. My parents had sent me some money via American Express, but it hadn't arrived. I felt I should stay quiet and think of a plan; I was in great need of one. My brain was free of all narcotics, hashish, and hallucinogens, and I made a promise to God that I would not put myself in jeopardy again and would never go back to prison. My epiphany came. I was not a god, and I had dined poorly. I was a mere mortal.

I made a decision. I was not going to return to the States immediately. Nothing was waiting for me there, and I knew that I wouldn't be able to see Europe anytime soon, if ever again, and that I should take advantage of being there.

•◊•◊•

I set up my *office* in the Palace Hotel in Madrid, and spent time at the Prado studying Goya's painting, from his incarceration. It was a powerful, depth-charged work, and I identified with him. There was no charcoal in my cell, nor did I have any artistic talent, but I knew how he felt.

At the hotel, there were ex-spies, beat-up matadors, journalists, courtesans, landowners, and drifters like me. I decided to go back to Paris, walk the streets, sit on the left and right banks of the Seine and see what it was like being alone. I thought I would hitchhike *("auto-stop")* and meet people along the way. I'd read Jack Kerouac, and thought it was my time to go on the road.

I checked back into the hotel that I'd originally gone to, the one with the hookers and food, and tried both. My hair was long, and I was gaining my strength back, working out and doing exercises. I enjoyed sitting out late at night at the cafes, listening to English, French, and German, pretending it was the 1920s and Hemingway was there with F. Scott, Picasso, and all the others. I listened to the bells of Notre Dame, and imagined I could hear Van Gogh laughing and Cézanne cursing.

In a club, I met some jazz musicians from New York, and they said they were going up to Copenhagen to play a gig with Chet Baker. A light went on. I'd always wanted to go to Copenhagen and lie naked in Tivoli Gardens with a couple of Danish girls.

I hitchhiked through Belgium and Germany. The Autobahn scared me with its total lack of speed limits, and since I couldn't be choosy, I was hitchhiking with some people who drove as if they were on the Formula One circuit. I wound up in Lübeck and spent some time with Heidi and her sisters, and then I took the ferry across into Copenhagen. They had great smörgåsbord on the boat. I listened to jazz and talked and talked.

In Copenhagen, I went through the main train station, where they were selling foot-long hotdogs with sauerkraut—a flashback to Nathan's in Coney Island and growing up. They were delicious.

The people were extremely friendly. You could feel their physicality; the Danes were a beautifully emotional people. In America, people were more standoffish, but here people were embracing, holding hands, kissing in public—they were more romantic, more alive. I was tall and dark-haired, and I stood out. Women would come over and talk to me and be quite aggressive, not knowing I was a sex maniac. It was a very easy feeling. Jazz artists like Dexter Gordon and black singers were welcomed with open arms. Also, they were very liberal about drugs. They didn't hassle people. I spent time in the clubs doing the things people do in a cosmopolitan city like that—smoking dope, drinking cognac, and listening to the fine jazz. I wondered if I could live there if things didn't work out for me in the States, and what I might do there. I had no occupation, except for thief and ex-con.

By this time, I was deeply tanned and had long hair. Danish women touched my hair and asked me if I would like to take a walk in the gardens. I enjoyed several nights under the tulips, but I found out that you couldn't register or check into a hotel with a woman who was not your wife. I couldn't figure that out. I'm still not sure why, since they were so much into free love.

The months were slipping by, and my money was dwindling. I was sorry to leave.

•◊•◊•

My homecoming from Europe was dismal. I flew in on a cargo plane—like in the Army. When I arrived I saw my parents' faces through the glass at JFK as I was taken into a side room to be strip-searched—my mother in tears, my father remaining stoic as usual. My passport was stamped by Interpol, and I was identified as a smuggler. I felt humiliated.

When we got to the house, I excommunicated myself to the basement. I didn't think I was capable of living upstairs. I apologized and told them that things had gotten out of control. And for the first time, I realized what I had done to them, and what serious trouble I was in. I had no income, no job, and no future. I had, I thought, reached bottom, but I was still far from there.

They never asked me about prison. The subject was never brought up at all, it was simply too painful, but they did ask me what I was going to do.

"I'm going to take a little time and get my stomach back together," I said. "And then I'm going to go look for a job."

It was too hot and too cold in the basement. I found the bed uncomfortably soft for me, and I had to sleep on the floor. I had lucid nightmares featuring flashbacks of the red-eyed rat, who came to me often. I did a lot of reading—I got lost in the books. I took long walks on the Boardwalk, and reflected.

It struck me how precious my freedom was and how close life and death could be. I pondered all the pain I had caused my parents. There was no way I could ever make it up to them. I knew that if I didn't get out of that basement quickly, my mental health would deteriorate. Mr. Red-Eyes lived there, and the bed was sagging with all my memories of who I used to be, but was no longer. I thought about who might hire me, whether I should go back to school, and whether I could ever ask my parents for money again. It really was time to leave the nest. I had no financial backup, and I had to find someone who could take care of me until I could take care of myself.

There was something that troubled me, something I couldn't quite put my finger on.

Something had definitely helped me, gotten me out of that prison; something greater than I was had given me a second chance. I was not going to stain it. Time was of the essence, and I had to act fast.

I made a few quick trips to Manhattan, but I came back quickly—it was too much for me.

My parents were supportive, but I didn't have a car. And my apartment was gone. I tried to touch base with some of my friends, but Jerry Cole was the only one I could find, and he was now paralyzed from heroin. Nobody knew what had happened to Fritzie.

My dad and I went to talk to Weenie's father, one of the most painful conversations that I've ever had. Weenie was still in jail, but he was a bad penny that would keep coming back. I had to reimburse his dad for the car we crashed—one of the rented cars we'd given away.

•◊•◊•

I was desperate to call Francesca. What reaction would I get? Would she hang up on me? I'd gone all the way to Europe to find her, and now I was craving her. I felt paranoid about people whispering about me. Since my story had been in the newspapers, I was afraid to go out with any of the local girls. My mind was made up. I would call Francesca, hopefully find her again, and see if she felt the same way about me that I felt about her.

It made sense at the time because it seemed to offer more possibilities than any other option. I needed to move on... in some feasible direction.

Chapter 5:

From the Valley to the Penthouse

I sat in the basement on the sagging bed, trying to get a grasp on what was ahead for me. I picked the phone up and dialed three numbers. Then I put it down. What if she hung up on me? But then why *should* she hang up on me? I'd done nothing wrong—to her. I dialed a few more numbers, then hung up. I'd never gone to Rome to meet her. I'd kept calling her and saying I was on the way. Maybe I never really wanted to go.

I realize now that I hung back because I didn't know how to deal with her. What did I have to offer her? It was my excuse to go to Europe. But if I had really wanted to, I would have seen her. And then the jewel heist... and prison. How could I even face her?

That night, a cat must have come past the window in the basement and peered in. I woke up, startled, and was sure it was Rudy, that pesky rat, coming for me. I went into the bathroom to piss, grabbed the toilet seat, and threw up. My legs shook, and my eyes burned. What I'd escaped finally hit me hard. I had a restless night, what was left of it, and dialed Francesca's number. I was expecting her to hang up on me, since I'd promised to come see her and didn't but just kept calling from all those cities. I never did hear anything from her and figured she was through with me, that I was simply a fling.

Yet she was sort of my teacher in the beginning: of literature, art, culture, folkways, and the mores of the bluebloods. She told me to throw away my T-shirts, my sweatsocks, and grow up. It was exciting, interesting, and challenging to be exposed to different cultures. Things that I'd read in books came alive. I think I knew that if I didn't drink deeply of the wine, I wouldn't get to drink again.

I'd been with her, and I knew what was there, but I was truly a sex addict. And to see the naked women on the beaches of St. Tropez, and the wildness of the Costa Brava, and the clubs of Torremolinas, and the hippies in Tangiers, and the beautiful women in Paris and London... Yes!

Nonetheless, I knew that she had returned to the States with her mother while I was in jail, so I made the call and used our private password. As much as she didn't want to admit it, there was electricity across the wire.

"So glad to hear from you!" she said. "Please come see me. I've missed you! I want to hear the story. Come into the city now. We need to talk."

•◊•◊•

I took my last twenty bucks and took the Long Island Railroad to New York City. I sat in a bar near 42nd Street, drinking a cheap beer and waiting to meet her. I knew it was time to be decisive. I looked down the aisle along the bar. There was a one-armed guy trying to get oysters into his mouth, who kept flopping them into the cocktail sauce. Every time he missed, he looked at the ceiling and said, "Praise the Lord!" There was also a black man with a bowtie and a brown derby, a Charlie McCarthy puppet, and a sign on the dummy that read "Us dummies need to eat." He had a tin cup. I drank my beer and ate my oysterettes. I was back in New York. I'd landed in sanity—or had I?

Francesca walked in, looking ravishing, with a deep tan, and we moved to the back, to a booth. We embraced, and she dropped a twenty and said, "Let's have some dinner."

I told her everything, and we had a tearful exchange. I don't think she understood what I went through, and her summer was right out of *Town and Country* magazine. One of the servants quit, King Constantine had a big party, they were filming another movie around the corner....

After I'd had a few Johnny Walkers and eaten dinner, she grabbed me by the arm and said, "Let's go to Park Avenue. I'll be your maid!"

We went to her empty maid's room on Park Avenue.

I think now that Francesca probably forgave me immediately—as soon as I called. I think she was restless and knew she could run with me. We could stay up all night, all day, do anything.

For me there was no going back, because there was nothing there to go back to, except that old saggy bed in the basement.

A few days later after seeing Francesca, I stared into Lenny Bruce's eyes and watched him roll up his sleeve and shoot up. Lenny was going out with Julie, one of Francesca's friends. She was a hooker and had introduced me to Lenny. He talked about how the government was so deeply into everybody's life, listening in on the phones, illegal spying, invading Vietnam, and how the people who were protecting our country were really not. It was all based on a lie, and he called it "The PR of the Princes and the Feudal Kingdoms." He said that they harassed him at his shows, and even though he was vulgar, he was telling the truth, and they wouldn't allow him to tell the truth.

I saw a man slipping down into the abyss. He went into the bathroom, rolling up his sleeve. Julie went in, too. He came out with his eyes glazed, his head tilted, and tucked himself into the corner of the couch, mumbling about "power to the people," and "let my people go." He asked me if I wanted some. I shook my head and just watched. I didn't even have a joint with me. I wanted to be clear. I know I missed the nuances, but Lenny was one of my heroes.

The floor in the Hotel Earle ran downhill. I guess in its day it was a grand little hotel. I had a suite, where people that Francesca and I picked up on the street slept in the front living room. I was just staying there for a few nights with Francesca before we got married. I slept all day, and got up when it was dark. We went down to the Fat Black Pussycat Cafe to play some chess or go to the Hip Bagel for dinner or breakfast. I used to put my feet in the fountain in Washington Square and smoke a joint. Marijuana was not my drug of choice, but everybody had it, so we smoked it. The park was full of kids from the 'burbs, panhandlers, old-time hipsters, new-time hipsters, flower children, power children, and doctors, and lawyers from NYU. Maybe Marty Scorsese was sitting right there with his feet in the water, too, when he was in film school. A few years later, Oliver Stone must have sat there, as well, after he left his red room.

One day, I sat near the fountain with Jerry Cole and Larry Rivers' son, as Rivers talked about the meaning of the word "is." Rivers was a leading artist at the time—an angry and intelligent man, a cool dude. He was lecturing us on getting on with our lives, how we should stop being bums. The days drifted into nights, and then into weeks. I listened to a lot of folk music by the Byrds and other up-and-coming groups. I'm trying to remember where we ate. I don't. We were all so high we didn't need food.

I was on Barrow Street with Jerry, and Hollingshead was there—he was one of the guys who brought the acid from England. We were sitting around in someone's living room, when the hipster rolled his sleeve up, put a rubber tourniquet around his arm, found a vein, and my friend Jerry started cooking up some heroin on a spoon over a candle.

I said, "What the fuck are you guys doing?"

"You want some?" they asked.

I said, "If I need it that bad that I've got to shoot it into my arm, then something's wrong."

They said, "Something's wrong." They started to nod their heads and drool.

I said, "I'm leaving, guys. This is boring."

But they said, "No, no, we'll drop you off."

We walked out and got in a cab to 42nd Street. We went into one of those midnight movies, and while we were sitting up there in this scummy, dirty movie house, in unison, like an orchestra, they both started throwing up. I ran out of the theater, smoked a joint in the alley, then had five hotdogs and an orange soda at Grants on 42nd Street.

I remember seeing a lot of movies in art theaters. At 103 MacDougal, Mary Travers lived on the top floor with her baby, and Nole and Petey Yarrow were just getting started. The Byrds were burning, Coltrane was playing. Sunday afternoon at Washington Square, chess, joints, peace not war, people in the fountain pool without their shoes, kids sleeping under trees, kids from the 'burbs coming in to score some pot, sharks swimming down from Harlem and Brooklyn to eat up the kids and spit them out, taking their money and giving them swag.

•◇•◇•

Prison took me to the fork in the road, and I took the wrong path. I wound up back into drugs again, but it was the '60s, so nobody noticed. It was hard to stay clean because it was everywhere, on every street corner, in every little club. After dark, you could smell the marijuana in the air. In Central Park, Tompkins Square, or Washington Square, everybody was high.

I wasn't in love, I was in lust, and I was curious. I wanted more. I wanted to walk on the wild side, and I was starting to feel godlike again. I thought I'd made the right turn. I had the security of wealth and power behind me. No one could hurt me. I had vowed never again to wind up broken in a jail cell.

•◇•◇•

I knew Francesca and her family wouldn't let me down—especially if I sired beautiful children. Once she was pregnant, they would have to take me—for better or worse. And she agreed: *let's make a beautiful child.* But we decided it would be best if we were married. At first, she couldn't conceive, and we went to a doctor. A few months after that, it just happened.

Francesca had a long list of disappointments. She'd had a tough childhood, without a father, and she was told she could do whatever she wanted because she belonged; she was an *us.* She thought she was different from everybody else, and entitled. She heard that her whole life. Her mother told her that men were horrible, evil, and all they wanted to do was use you. Her mother became a lesbian later in life.

I didn't know what I was getting into, but I was still having constant flashbacks of the red-eyed rat and prison, and since I was drugging and whoring again, I figured marriage to Francesca would insulate me from being jailed a second time. I didn't want to marry a rich Jewish princess from my background. I wanted to step up. I liked moving among the really rich and powerful, and this was my ticket. I thought marriage was solid: you get married, and that's it. Like my parents. And then you grow into a relationship.

And I needed security. I was scared.

Chapter 6:

Walking the Line

I was at the gym with Jimmy Hamburger at the Algonquin Hotel. Jimmy worked in the garment district and came from Boston, so we had something in common. I asked him to find me a justice of the peace. I told him I was going to marry Francesca.

He said, "You're going to do what? How can you marry her? I have a great tip on a horse tomorrow. It's a lock." Jimmy Hamburger was a degenerate gambler.

Later, he said, "I found a justice of the peace across from the racetrack. I set it up so you can get married an hour before we go to the track."

I don't know how I got Francesca to do it. I told her I had a tip on a horse and that Jimmy was going to meet me at the track. Would she like to come along? She said, "Yes, why not."

She couldn't wait to spite her mother. She was having a fight with her that week, plus her sister was getting married in a few days to Dr. Bellin. We had a quick ceremony, and then I went off to bet the daily double. Jimmy was best man, of course. And he did win the double. Were we high? Yes, indeed, we were high. Why should that day be different from any other day? In the *New York Times*, when they wrote about the wedding, they referred to me as a "young importer." I was indeed an importer of fine goods from Morocco. I spent my wedding night at my friend Charlie Aug's house, on his sofa. I drifted off to sleep thinking, *What did I do?*

•◊•◊•

I was at the Carib Hilton in Puerto Rico, married to Francesca. Her mother and my father sent us on our honeymoon. We sat by the pool, smoking one joint after another, talking about a future that sounded like nonsense.

We flew back to New York with no place to live, so we checked into the Sutton East Hotel on East 56th Street; it was time for me to get a job. The illusion of marriage lasted about a week, until she went to get some drugs from a friend of mine. She implied that she did more than drugs. Right then I should have called it a day, but I wanted to have children, and it was my time. In the '60s, people got married in their early twenties; it was the thing to do. After the first week, I knew the rules. She played her ace, but I kept my hand close and went along with my plan: marry money, marry up, marry into a rich European family. The French have their mistresses, the Italians have their mistresses, the Mexicans have their luncheon girlfriends. And that's the way it was. I had nothing to lose. I'd already changed my mind more than once: in prison, in Africa, and, thanks to Tim Leary, in Cambridge.

I believed that I could turn this into a positive experience. I would get a job, I would make a ton of money, I would raise a family, and my parents would be proud of me since I was no longer a jailbird. And it worked; I made a lot of money renting and selling apartments and leasing furniture. And Francesca did have a trust fund. I found a magnificent apartment. I had everything I could want. I just didn't know that there were no brakes on that train, and I couldn't just get off. I was addicted to the fast life, to action, and I couldn't stop.

And you have babies. And bills. There were lessons to be learned. And now, in the Crystal City, I can look back on it and say that I did it. I played the game. Not everyone gets out. A lot of my friends, acquaintances, hitchhiking buddies, fellow prisoners, and Botany Club members are dead.

Would I do it again the way I did it? I don't know.

I think that things could have gone along as they were going and we probably wouldn't have divorced, if the Contessa hadn't wanted to ruin Francesca's life. She wanted her to be alone, bitter, and angry—just like her. She thought if I was gone, she could control bringing up the children and punish Francesca for the rest of her life.

And that's exactly what she did.

•◇•◇•

The Contessa remarried, this time to an Argentine importer of fine goods from Colombia—a cocaine dealer. The Contessa then helped her daughter open up a fancy jewelry store on Madison Avenue, called "Francesca's"—with just enough money to fail.

The Contessa did make sure that our children would be well taken care of and that the lineage was set up before she tried to get rid of me. I'm sure some of the stories Francesca told her mother about what I was doing were unacceptable. But my shoes were under the bed, and I was being a good father, even as Francesca was carrying on in civilized adultery, the Italian way. After the first child, though, I was demoted to a lesser standing.

When I was twenty-seven, I went to the family doctor and told him I was getting stomach pains every time I called to talk to my wife. He gave me a prescription for these little blue pills, told me to take one a half-hour before I called her, and that was the beginning of my Valium addiction. It took me twenty years to finally decide to get off Valium, and then it took me three months and a lot of anxiety to do it.

I had a friend who was in the real estate business, and he seemed to be making a lot of money renting apartments in New York City. There was a recession, or they just couldn't fill the buildings up, and they needed rental agents. If you didn't already have a license, you needed someone to sponsor you to get your license, with much study involved. Well, it was time for me to get a job, so I wound up working in Queens, in Jackson Heights, underneath the elevated train, getting sponsored by an old, crazy Italian who had strange people working in the office. It took about three weeks before I was eligible to take my real estate broker's test. The Contessa owned a little sports car in

Manhattan that still had Roman plates on it, and I drove it from the hotel, back and forth to work, waiting to take my test.

Francesca's mother acquired two Jewish sons-in-law in one week. Her robber baron great-grandfather probably turned over in his grave. Two Jews in one week. As I entered the church on 71st and Madison, the St. James Church, where some years later my eldest son would get married, I was ushered into the first row in the wedding ceremony of Christina and Howard. I slid in, sat down, and the man next to me extended his hand and said, "How do you do, I'm Senator Jack Javits." And I thought, *I'm Barry the crook, fresh out of jail. Glad we could share this pew. By the way, aren't you Jewish, too?* I was sitting next to a legendary New York senator.

The church was full of dignitaries, industry leaders, models, actors, restaurateurs, and Italian designers. Afterwards, we went to the reception at the Contessa's huge Park Avenue apartment. My head was spinning. There were people whose names I'd seen or heard on television, in newspapers, and in movie magazines. We were eating chopped liver together—and other canapés.

•◊•◊•

After I got my real estate license, it was time to get our first pad. We got a small, one-bedroom apartment on 61st Street between Park and Lexington. My neighbor was the bald-headed Otto Preminger, and across the street lived Lee Remick.

All I needed was a job.

My buddy Joe Russo and I opened up a small company on 51st Street and 2nd Avenue, called Duke Management, named after my German shepherd. Our first building was a house on 51st Street. It was owned by the Greenbergs, two Jewish refugees. Mrs. Greenberg looked like Porky Pig's brother, and Mr. Greenberg had a walrus moustache. They gave us a desk, a phone, a whole ream of blank real estate board leases, and a typewriter. I'd failed typing in high school because of dyslexia, and I didn't know how I would type those leases, if I could ever rent anything. There was dust everywhere, the one hundred forty apartments weren't finished, the kitchens and bathrooms were being installed. But we put an ad in the paper, and the next Saturday morning they started to come. From the suburbs, from the Village, from Jersey and Connecticut, they all wanted to have a little place in New York.

I hadn't done any selling since my days in the Army when I was selling used cars instead of being a soldier. I had joined the Reserves three years earlier in 1964, to avoid being drafted, and I was in the 77th Division in New York. They sent me to basic training in Fort Dix, where most of my unit was made up of guys from Coney Island, Bensonhurst, and other parts of Brooklyn. They were mainly Italian kids, and their families owned bars, restaurants, and businesses there. I really enjoyed their company. They had plenty of cash and gold chains and knew how to pay off our sergeants and our training personnel to get favors. We were in the old Third Training Regiment in the wooden barracks with basically no heat—it was like living outdoors. I didn't have any trouble adjusting to basic training, and learning that the spirit of the bayonet is to kill. They made us take rifles, pistols, and machine guns apart until we could do it with our eyes closed. And then they moved us out into tents in winter. We lay in cold water, fired our weapons at targets, and ate slop out of pans in the rain.

When we got out of basic training, we were able to get our first weekend passes. I worked for a supply sergeant, Sergeant Sherman. We went into Wrightstown the first week, and he had a little used car business, selling to the soldiers. He let me off and said he was going to have a few beers, and he would bring me back a hero sandwich. Could I watch the lot of cars for a few hours while he played pool? He came back as it was getting dark. I had sold three cars. He couldn't believe the pile of cash in front of me, and I was smoking one of his cigars with my feet up on the desk. Each week after that, he'd drive me into town and give me one of the cars to use, and I spent the next couple of months selling used cars and playing poker.

Well, here I was now, married, renting out apartments, and working for myself. I remember my first customer. She was a divorcée fighting with her husband. She needed an apartment right away. There were a few that were model apartments, and I was told not to rent them. But, regardless, I convinced her to rent one of the model apartments and pay one hundred a month over what they were asking because it was furnished. I also asked her to sign a blank lease, and surprisingly, she did, providing me with all the necessary references and money. The next day, the Greenbergs came in. I gave them the money and the blank lease. As a lawyer, he wondered how I got someone to do that. But when he saw the overage, his greed was evident. I went on to rent the entire building without getting any of the leases typed right away. I was young and inspired confidence, so I got tenants to sign blank leases at the moment of closing. I had to, because, being dyslexic, I couldn't type them myself; I just had someone else type them the following week. After I filled up another building, we engaged other landlords who were in trouble.

As the money poured in we hired other people to work for us, and had a good business going. Then Joe decided to bring in his father, who was a siding salesman and very oily. I didn't want him around, and I decided it was time to move on. *Goodbye, Duke, you can have it.*

I had a salesman working with me, and we opened up a new office on 57th and 2nd. My uncle owned the building and gave me a very cheap lease, but we outgrew that in about two months and moved into a fancy building on the first floor at 57th and 1st, across from a good deli.

Francesca and I moved into an apartment on 63rd, between 5th and Madison. It belonged to a friend of mine from Long Island, John Schweitzer. He was a good guy and he was buying a house, so we took over his furnished apartment in an elegant townhouse on the ground floor.

When Francesca became pregnant, it was time to move again. We got a beautiful two-bedroom, two-bath on the 35th floor of a new building. You could see for miles around.

The business was growing, and I was starting to meet more and more interesting people. My new partner on 57th Street was a sleazy guy from the Bronx who claimed he was a descendent of a wealthy Eastern European family, and he was a karate expert. He was always throwing poses. He was a good schmoozer, but I knew it was temporary, and I needed some help where I could control the situation.

As the business continued to grow, he brought in a friend of his to be the accountant, whom I really liked. He had the same name as a big clothier: Stanley Blacker. He was from Queens, married to his high school sweetheart, a CPA, an attorney, and an alcoholic. And he loved to fish, as I did. Francesca and I were involved with fixing up the new apartment, furnishing it, getting it ready, making new friends, and having parties, all while her belly grew. Our business kept expanding, and my partner was misbehaving by drinking during the day and chasing tenants— not that I wasn't doing that, too, but he wasn't there when he needed to be there. He moved to Sutton Place when he couldn't afford to, and forgot to show up to work on time. Stanley saw the numbers growing, and I decided that we were going to move to an even larger space on 49th, an entire floor we called *Creative Leasing*. We went in, Stanley and I, and gave a small room to a little guy named Harold, the Deputy Commissioner of Air Pollution.

We took a floor in a brownstone owned by an old Sicilian lunatic on top of a fine French restaurant. Now there was a breeding ground for lunatics. The cast sleeping on my couch included *the* Rodney Sheldon, otherwise known as Harvey Sheldon; Slick Jimmy Hamburger, who looked like a small James Caan; *the* Bruce Watkins, and later, such eminent people as Maddie Paddy; Trish, Sonia, Tina, and many local characters from down the block, particularly the Pussycat, which was frequented by bookmakers and hustlers.

•◇•◇•

My first son was born on January 20, ten pounds six—a big boy. Getting to the hospital was almost a problem because that was the year we had the brownout in New York. All the power went off. It was '66, and we were on the 35th floor. Fortunately, the lights came on the next day when we took Francesca to Doctor's Hospital. At the hospital, the Contessa was congratulating my mother and father at the baby's size, the fact that it was a male, and how pink and perfect he was—and how the legacy would live on. Well done! Good job! When the moyel and the rabbi showed up, my wife fainted at the briss. We would live there comfortably for the next year, as Creative Leasing developed.

I went down to the nursery. It was the day of the first Super Bowl. I was proud and felt that everything I'd gone through had been worthwhile. My parents' faces were lit up. I felt that I'd paid them back for some of the pain I'd given them. My dad was handing out cigars, my mother was cheery, and Francesca was bragging. We all decided that Alexander the Great should be named that day—Alexander Stuart, after her brother, whom nobody talked about. No one seemed to know exactly what happened to him, but Francesca wanted to honor him.

Having a child was a job to Francesca. It was my job, too, and I got straight A's in this college—even amidst lots of dinner parties, lots of theater, and lots of interesting people. We were having such a good time with our first child we decided to have a second one right away and raise a family.

•◇•◇•

The following year, another boy was born, and the aging Contessa cheered again, even harder. Yes, another boy! Christopher. Same room, January 12. We didn't make it to the Super Bowl. The year after that, April 20, it was Tony's turn. He had to be induced, and was 11 pounds, 6 ounces, with a full head of hair. He couldn't fit in the bassinette. He drained the bottle quickly and screamed—keeping all the other babies up. Francesca's mother was banging the table; another boy! She was drunk that day.

At that point, I went into the furniture business. We figured if we could furnish New York apartments, we could get stewardesses and airline personnel. It worked perfectly. We would go out to the airports and give lectures and they would come pouring in. Pan American, American, Swissair, TWA.... My office looked like an airline terminal, with everyone in uniforms. The money was great and the scenery was highly appealing. Then temptation arrived. Fortunately or unfortunately, these deals worked late into the night; stewardesses arriving on international flights wouldn't get up until four in the afternoon to come over, and we usually had to sell them furniture and deliver it in the evenings. We made sure they were happy and had a good time in New York City.

One day, Francesca's mother asked me to meet her at the Majestic, on 72nd Street and Central Park West. Her friend from Brown, Harris, and Stevens had a listing that I should look at.

The building was across from the Dakota, which is one of the landmarks of New York. I remember the three of us going up to apartment 16C East. Two apartments on the floor opened up to a double height living room, thirty by forty feet, with a view of Central Park and a wrap-around terrace. Four bedrooms. A huge kitchen. The Contessa looked around, put her finger to her jaw, looked up at the wood-burning fireplace and all the closets and said, "This will do."

She made out a check for $120,000, and we signed the contract. I gave it to the teller at our bank and asked him to cash it. Everybody looked at me. I said, "I'm just joking. Please deposit it." We came back to the apartment to show it to Francesca a few days later. I knocked on the door, and an Arabic-looking man opened it, wearing a ripped T-shirt and a dirty pair of khakis, his hair a mess.

"I'm Barry Hornig and this is my wife, Francesca. We'd like to look at the apartment again and take some measurements. We bought it."

He looked at me furiously. "Who the hell do you think I am, the janitor? I'm Elia Kazan!" We both were a little taken aback at his gruffness. "My wife has a headache," he said. "Just knock on the door and she'll go under the covers, and you can measure the bedroom."

His wife was Barbara Loden of *Splendor in the Grass*, Warren Beatty's first movie with Natalie Wood. If I had stayed in Emerson College studying theater and fine arts, maybe I would have succeeded in film. But I didn't have the perseverance—or probably the talent.

•◇•◇•

The room had teak bookcases all around. Unfortunately, we didn't have enough books to fill them. There were double-height windows facing the park and a thirty-foot wrap-around terrace right off the kitchen. The study was full of energy, ideas, passion, and fire. It turned out that a number of amazing people had spent time in this apartment. When Brando and Lee J. Cobb and Rod Steiger all sat in that room with Budd Schulberg, tossing around their stories, the power must have been palpable. *On the Waterfront* is still one of my favorite movies. I would have loved to have listened to the conversations. The apartment had magic in it. I later learned that Elia Kazan wrote *The Arrangement* in that room. Marilyn Monroe had also been there with her husband, Arthur Miller.

Underneath me lived Frank Costello, the Don of Dons, the head of the New York Mafia. He liked to sleep in the afternoons, so he asked us please not to have the baby driving his Big Wheels then. He wasn't there all the time, but Al, the doorman, would say, "Mr. H? Mr. C's here. The maids should put the Big Wheels away. Put duct tape on the kids' mouths and handcuff them—or take them out to the park, immediately."

The Don dressed magnificently, with camel hair coats, and would take Francesca out in his limousine once in a while, when she went out shopping. I don't think he liked me. I was *very* polite to him, though—*always*. But he gave me that look: You'd better be nice to the Italian you're married to—or else!

My dream apartment in New York City had silk drapes, Nettle Creek plush velvet cushions, and Bloomingdale's furniture. The maids, the servants, the sheepdogs, and the bills arrived. The apartment itself was a trap, as beautiful and alluring as it was.

I met the men from Plaza Management, which was owned by Alex DiLorenzo and Sol Goldman, who were the largest landlords in New York City. Supposedly they started in Brooklyn, in a candy store, with a cigar box full of cash. I never believed that story. I became familiar with their agents, who were former prizefighters, Italian-Americans, Irishmen, and ex-cops. Goldman and DiLorenzo gave me their apartments, which ranged from junk to exclusive high-rise buildings, and asked me to fill them up. Since we knew many stewardesses, it was pretty easy to do business there. But they had too many apartments. There weren't enough stewardesses in the world to fill all their buildings, and New York was still largely under rent stabilization, which meant you could only raise the rent when somebody moved out. The stewardesses were good, but we needed something better.

Chapter 7:

Living the High Life

By 1966, I had three young children in diapers, a French maid, an Italian wife, and I was on top of the world. Still, I didn't speak French, so I didn't know what my wife and the maid were talking about. But that was Joséphine, the day maid. Then we had the night maid and the nanny.

They came from England, they came from Israel, they came from France, they came from Switzerland, to be interviewed. They had letters, recommendations, and stories.

Those days were long. Very little sleep. Days ran into nights, but that was the best time. I loved my children. I loved smelling the powder, kissing them, holding them, watching them grow, reading Dr. Seuss books, waking up on Christmas morning and putting three sets of everything together, constructions: it was great. Since we lived on Central Park West, when the Thanksgiving Parade came by, everybody came over. Christina's friends, my friends, Sid and Gail Lumet, the Stookies, people who had children in expensive schools, like the École Française, which is where my kids went to school. My wife spoke French and the maid spoke French; now my kids spoke French. I went to recitals in French, with my gun in my shoulder holster, another pistol in my boot, and a stack of hundreds in my other boot.

It was ten degrees, three small kids, wind blowing, a 120-pound old sheepdog, double stroller, off to the children's zoo.

"Good morning, John."

"Good morning, Barry. Are you off?"

"Yes, we're off to the park to see *Alice in Wonderland*."

That was my neighbor, John Lennon, who lived across the street from me in the Dakota. Most mornings, I met him getting a newspaper.

We were just neighborly, and I never did get around to telling him about my adventures in Span and Tangiers, or about my scheme to bring him product... At that point, with two kids in a baby carriage, I didn't think it would be appropriate. "I got locked up because I wanted to get dope for you!" I think he would have found it funny, but it was enough that he said hello.

The zoo at Central Park, bears, the cafeteria, the monkey house. I was one of the few dads without his spouse.

I had two nephews, Marco and Andy Bellin. On any Sunday, we went to Rappaports, on 2nd Avenue near the Fillmore Theater. The waiters would run out as we entered, and try to give us money not to come in. There's only one thing I could say—"Food fight!" They gave you these tasty little rolls with cream cheese and herring, and with five boys, an Israeli mother's helper, and me, we didn't care what happened. We paid the tab, and the kids had a good time. We took extra tables and tipped the waiters to leave them empty, so people would stay away from us.

Howard Johnson's on Broadway knew us. Fein and Shapiro on 72nd Street feared us. "Here they come!"

•◊•◊•

When we boarded the *Cristoforo Colombo*, the Italian liner, the kids were ages three, four and five. *We* were me, Betsy, my gorgeous mother's helper, my wife, and, of course, the Contessa—together for the trip of a lifetime. First class to Naples, and then on to a villa in Rome. Sitting up on the deck, watching the ship pull out, I flashed back to a few years before when they had thrown me off the boat. Now, I was next door to the Captain's cabin, sitting at his table. I guess I had arrived.

We sat at the Captain's table with the kids, who all had wind-up toys. "G is for gorilla." "B is for boy." We tried to keep them under control, but there were a lot of aristocrats in those days who cruised across the ocean, and they were not in good moods, being hung over in the morning. There was a lot of complaining to the Captain and the crew about the noise we made, but the complaints went nowhere, because the Contessa's family owned a huge portion of stock in the company that owned the boat we were sailing on. Nobody swam in the pool in first class, but my kids broke that custom.

Three days into the voyage, as we passed the Azores, we caught the tail end of a hurricane off the coast of Spain. Even the crew was turning green. Everyone on the ship had to be tied down in their cabins, and was sick—except for me, my mother's helper, and my three sons. We had the run of the ship. They thought they were at an amusement park, sliding up and down with the waves. It was the best. Up forty feet, down forty feet, up forty feet, down forty feet.

We had three rooms together next to the Captain's cabin. Three kids in one room, Francesca and me in another, and her mother in the corner room. They couldn't figure out who I was with, and it was fun. Musical beds and chairs.

Arriving in Naples, then driving to Rome, driving up the *Via Aventina*, a few blocks from the Colosseum, was beautiful *Porta Latina*. We couldn't stay at the big house—it was rented to King Constantine from Greece, the permanent resident. The guest house had three bedrooms and a swimming pool. Since the King was cruising somewhere around the Greek Islands, I had a tour of the big house. On the walls were Cézannes, Matisses, Van Goghs, Renoirs—apparently William Spaulding had advised William Frick on his acquisitions for the Frick Museum. He was a great connoisseur of French art. He kept a few for himself, donating the rest to the Boston Museum of Fine Art.

•◇•◇•

The day before Christmas in 1968, we rented a large corporate apartment to an advertising agency. The check for rent and security was substantial, but we soon learned it was no good. The head of the advertising company informed us he had no more funds. He was keeping two girls and his wife at the same time, and was a fraud and a scoundrel. But he did have a truckload of Cleopatra Bath Oil. The oil that made the Egyptians' skin silky. My right-hand man, Jimmy Hamburger, told me he knew where we could get rid of this swag for cash. But we had to rent a truck. We went to Queens, rented a trailer truck, and went over to the warehouse on the Lower West Side where it was stored, and had it loaded. There we were, the day before Christmas, with a truck full of bath oil—not exactly legal tender. We went around the docks, where there were people, bums and assorted derelicts around fires in cans, trying to keep warm. We were waiting for our connection to arrive to pay us cash for the truckload. I went to eat. When I got back, Jimmy had opened the back of the truck, and was selling the Cleopatra as a combination of bath oil and alcohol. The lines were around the block. People came back two hours later, drunk with bubbles coming out of their mouths.

Christmas Eve. Bums belching bubbles. Never leave Jimmy Hamburger alone with a whole bottle, but he was very good at pulling a heist.

After our first son was born, I became second in importance to Francesca. By the time our third son arrived on the scene I was almost an afterthought. Since Francesca was a half-Italian, half-American aristocrat, she informed me of the way things were in Paris and Rome: you lived your charm-filled life, taking care of your family, and you made it appear that everything was fine. And she did what she wanted to, and I did what I wanted to. True, I was doing this before I learned her aristocratic style. And so was she. It was what people now call an open marriage. It wasn't what I was raised with, but then again, growing up, I didn't know anybody who had parents who were divorced.

It started on Fire Island, when the sea planes came and went. She was alone there all week, and I was in the Majestic alone all week. I was surrounded by temptation, and so was she.

We took exotic vacations, and never had screaming fights in front of the kids—actually, we hardly fought. Two different ships going in two different directions, though my shoes were under the bed, and I always came home.

It was getting uncomfortable, however, with the guns in

my closet, boxes of hundred dollar bills, and the constant drug sales in my buildings. The cash was from renting apartments and getting exorbitant fees for putting "undesirable" people in buildings all over Manhattan. And I was working with the boys. I was "a friend of theirs," the pimps, the prostitutes, and the stewardesses.

I was trying to hold it all together, and it appeared that it *was* together. I had a beautiful family, wonderful pictures, lots of time with my kids and my sheepdog, houses in the country, trips to the Caribbean, trips to Europe. I didn't hurt anybody. I tried to be very discreet and careful.

At the top of the lake at Upper St. Regis in the Adirondacks was a rustic house called Treetops—an original Adirondack. It was owned by a charming, gray-haired lady called Marjorie Merriweather Post, the heir to Post cereals and the wealthiest woman in America. Her daughter was Dina Merrill, the actress who married Cliff Robertson. Every Friday night she'd have a hundred of her closest friends over, twenty-five for dinner, and then the rest would arrive, and we would square dance all night. On certain nights, she would have first-run movies before they were shown in theaters. Before my first square dancing experience at Mrs. Post's house, we had a highly engaging dinner party. There were her chosen twenty-five people with her at the head of one table, and I sat at the other end. Behind each of us was a butler, which made me very nervous. They would lean in when I started to touch something.

To my left was an interesting, weathered general, who was telling stories about himself and George Patton during the war, and Patton's cowardly dog. Nothing disparaging, just stories. I learned subsequently that General McAuliffe was present when Patton broke through to relieve the surrounded airborne troops. The Panzer division asked McAuliffe if he would surrender, and his reply was, "Nuts!"

Four chairs down on the right were Dina Merrill and Cliff Robertson, who also joined in the square dancing later. On my right, a few chairs down, was U.S. Sen. Joe Tidings from Maryland. He was one of Jack Kennedy's close friends and confidantes. He was telling exciting football stories, sailing stories, fraternity house stories. I looked into his eyes and saw the new frontier.

He was one of *them*. Handsome, strong, intelligent, with good breeding, and he wanted to make a difference. I was proud to be in his company.

The rest of the people were from the camps up there, and had been coming for years for the square dancing. They all had a little touch of that East Coast accent that was in the movies in the 20s and 30s. Everything was "darling," "spectacular," and "top drawer." I don't really remember what I said or whom I talked to. A sip of wine, a gulp of brandy, a small Caesar salad, a little fish. I listened more than I spoke because they had more to say than I did at the ripe age of twenty-nine, and I knew it. Afterward, we went into the living room, where there were professional dancers, men and women in cowboy hats and gingham shirts with scarves. They started off with a professional square dance emcee. It went on and on for hours, and it was fun. The other guests knew what they were doing because they'd been there before. They were almost professional. I tried my best, which wasn't good. But it was fun. For the people who didn't want to dance, there was another room, a theater. It looked like a small movie theater, and first-run movies were playing.

The only way to get to the island was by boat. There were chauffeurs with caps and jackets with Mrs. Post's crest on the uniforms, and on the beautiful, antique Garwood boats and Criss Crafts.

I remember the next day vividly. The sky was blue, the waves were a light chop. Ah, a day at the races. I was told that they were having an oh-boat race—an antique sailboat race. I grew up on powerboats, but I wasn't much of a sailor—except for the dinghy in summer camp.

My brother-in-law was up with his wife, and we decided that we were going to race. He was on the mainsail; he was Captain Courageous, and I was going to do all the dirty work. We took another one of the cousins on our boat, and went off to the starting line. Everybody was in beautiful costumes, all white scarves, hats, nautical colors. I wore my Jimi Hendrix outfit and felt out of place. A canon went off, and I almost fell overboard. I didn't know it was the start of the race, I thought we were being attacked. Off we went into the wind in the other boats' wake. Immediately we were in last place. Howard screamed, "Ready about!" and this big piece of wood came crashing toward me. I ducked, and then it went crashing the other way. *Damn! This is dangerous!*

The other boaters were singing sailing songs and moving along at a beautiful pace. We were going around in circles. We did finish—a half hour after everybody else. I was black-and-blue, my suedes were soaked and my beads were broken. They were giving out trophies. Howard and I got little buttons. I guess it was a consolation prize.

That evening, over a bottle of Chardonnay, my hands all burnt from handling the ropes, I thought maybe I'd become a professional sailboat racer. My type of sport. I liked the costumes. But, of course, both the Contessa and Francesca put us down, and told us we were hellacious and should stay on land. I suggested that Howard and I go out next week and put the Star of David on our boat. That didn't go over. The Contessa said, "Over my dead body," and I murmured to myself, "That could be arranged."

A few weeks later, one of Francesca's girlfriends—her best friend—was having a wedding in Palm Beach. We were invited, of course, and the wedding was at the Everglades Club. It was 1971, and the club had a restricted membership—no Jews.

The girl who was getting married was Susanne Atwater Kent, whose grandfather invented the Atwater Kent radio. Big Palm Beach money. Susanne was marrying Thomas Hitchcock, the great-grandson of Andrew Mellon, one of the pillars of American society.

The wedding was black tie, with a fabulous society orchestra, and the best food that money could buy. Tommy Hitchcock was the younger brother of Peggy Hitchcock, who was LSD king Tim Leary's sponsor and girlfriend. They lived in Millbrook, up the Hudson, in the famous "House of Acid."

We all went out after the wedding on Mr. Kent's one hundred twenty-foot private boat. It was an antique, one of those custom jobs made in the '30s. They had a small band playing in the back. In attendance were assorted heiresses from New York, Bartle Bull (who owned the *Village Voice),* Center Hitchcock, Billy Hitchcock and many loonies from upper-crust Woodstock, Philadelphia, Boston—top-drawer families.

This was before cocaine was fashionable. There was a lot of champagne, joints, and for the lucky who wanted it, window pane acid. I remember the sun setting into the ocean, going under the boat, coming back and rising, all in the space of ten minutes. I must have been very high.

The next day, I was in the spectacular landmark, magnificently decorated winter home of Mrs. Post, *Mar-A-Lago*. It turns my stomach to think that Trump lives there now. The thought that the Donald moved into that magnificent estate and flocked all the walls up makes me ill, and I'm sure I'm not the only one.

Tommy Hitchcock became the godfather of my son, Alex. It was a strange crowd, along with the intermarrying and the tripping. They didn't seem to want to be with us socially, and I didn't give a shit about them at all. They said "Oh, wow!" too many times. The next year, I think Peggy got married to Dr. Scoroni in a wedding in New York, and I got to visit with her. She was a very interesting, smart, cool lady. Later she gave me her penthouse on Park Avenue to sell for her.

I heard she ended up in a teepee in Arizona, in the red rock mountains of Sedona where she saw God—and where she died.

I was sitting one night at a dinner party at Christina's, Francesca's sister's home, and there was a banker, a lawyer, a starlet, a designer, and a painter. I came in late and had my leathers on. They were all in black tie and drag. They were Truman Capote, Loeb, Serge Semenenko, the innovative Hollywood banker, Katrina Millionaire and Andy Warhol, Halston and David Susskind, and Howard and Christina. They sat me next to this dark, attractive, voluptuous Greek girl. I was very high, and I talked about greasing my leathers and letting her slide all over me. We had a good laugh; her name was Christina also. I really didn't know who she was, but we were carrying on. I think she was pretty drunk, too. The next day, my Christina told me I'd better send a letter of apology—the woman around whom my conduct had been lewd and lascivious was Christina Onassis of the Onassis fortune.

After meeting these people and mixing with the high society, it's hard for me to be impressed with anything material. These were the families of the robber barons who controlled America. They built the railroads, they dug for oil, they manipulated, robbed, and cheated their way to the top, and today they're Chase Manhattan and the Mellon Bank. They sit on the boards of each other's companies, after having taken over the United States. It jaded me, as a young man who wasn't born into money, but I socialized with them and heard the stories. Some involved the Contessa.

When the Contessa was eighteen, Joe Kennedy came to court her, and her father threw him out of the house. Supposedly, she was about to be engaged to Henry Cabot Lodge, who was dating her at the time. She decided to go off to Europe with her brother on a cruise ship. They went around to all the ports of call—London, Le Havre, Naples—and in Rome, she met the dashing young Count. He was titled and handsome, with a castle and no money, as was the case for many Counts. I heard that, at this point, she was a prim and proper virgin colonial damsel. I think the Count must have slipped her the eel. Bells supposedly went off, stars lit up the sky, and she was in love. Subsequently, the Count married her, which was a scandal to everyone in Back Bay and Beacon Hill. You didn't marry greasy Italians, even if they were titled. They ran bakeries, and cooked food in restaurants, and had olive oil in their hair. This was the 1940s.

They had Christina, their first daughter, at the start of World War II, and Francesca a few years later in Switzerland. And even though they were under enormous pressure from Mussolini as World War II approached, I understood that the Count and the Contessa smuggled a lot of people out during the start of the Holocaust. I heard among them there were quite a few Jews, which was odd, considering the antisemitic remarks she had made to Jimmy Hamburger and me on one memorable, stormy night. Subsequently, they were chased out of or fled Italy, as the war got hot and the fighting ignited. They stayed in Geneva during the war and tried to help out. Both girls were sent to convent schools. Francesca said the nuns were abusive and whacked her.

After the war, they settled back in the villa. One afternoon the Contessa walked into her bedroom to find the Count breaking in the maid. He was banished from the house and the church, but they stayed married. The Count had a gallery near the Spanish

Steps, sold very expensive jewelry, and was a playboy. I have to admit that they treated him very nicely and respectfully, and I never heard a bad word about him. I got to meet him later, and I found him charming and entertaining. So it seems the Contessa had good reason to be the way she was, though she certainly milked it.

I didn't know Salvador Dalí was going to be among us when I was standing in line at a benefit for a children's charity at Roosevelt Raceway. At my table were my wife, Francesca, Dr. Bellin, Christina, to my left was an empty chair, and across from me were Andy Warhol, Edie Sedgwick, and Steve Paul, who owned the hottest club in town, The Scene, in Hell's Kitchen.

I didn't know Dalí was there, because his seat was empty. But I got up to place a bet, and a man was standing in front of me in a plumed hat, with a black cape over his shoulder, long gray hair, and the strangest waxed moustache. Under his left arm, he carried what appeared to be a little pussycat, but it was an ocelot with a diamond-studded collar and a velvet leash.

He got up to place his bet. And when they pushed the buttons for the tickets to come out, the ocelot hissed and started slapping at them as they emerged from the machine. I was too startled even to say anything. He turned to me and said, "I wish you luck."

After betting, I went back to the table, and there he was in the empty seat at the head of the table. He had chicken, and was feeding the ocelot, petting it, and wiping its mouth with a napkin. Andy Warhol sat across from him, wearing dark glasses, not paying attention to Salvador or the ocelot; he seemed to be in his own world. Edie was talking a mile a minute to Francesca and Christina. Steve Paul was very cool and laid back, and I visited with him.

Mr. Dalí asked me what I did; I told him I was in the real estate business, since I'd just gotten my license.

He blathered on about Madrid and Goya, and Goya being in prison, and how art was suppressed under Franco. He wasn't really talking to me; he was talking through me. He kept looking up with those eyebrows, and his eyes toward Heaven.

His accent was a little difficult for me, since I had had a few vodkas. The ocelot settled down in his lap and started to purr, which made me much calmer. But it was definitely interested in my filet of sole.

Andy was sketching things on napkins. I wish he had signed them. I would have grabbed some. People were saying, "Edie, eat!" but she didn't eat anything. She just kept babbling.

Dalí settled down and started humming. Andy started talking about the fourth dimension, special acrylic paints, soup cans, Nestlé's, and how it all had meaning to the birth of life.

I remember driving home after the party in a limousine, and Cricri (Christina) asked, "Barebare, did you have a good time with the cat?" I said, "Yes, Christina, it was quite an evening. Thank you for inviting me."

That was the only time I saw Dalí.

Chapter 8:
Changes Are a-Comin'

I truly did love Christina Paolozzi, Francesca's sister. She was a spirit above all. Her personality was vivacious and her face adorned many magazine covers in those years. She was the "Barechested Contessa." My mother-in-law punched Richard Avedon in the nose for publishing a nude picture of her in *Harper's Bazaar*. Yes, she did throw the best parties in New York, and she was in *La Dolce Vita*. She loved people, loved having them around—the opposite of my wife, who was a recluse, and found friendship and companionship in the words of authors, drugs... and well, yes, other men.

The first time I met Christina, she had a small apartment on 58th Street. I could see her beauty, untouched, with no makeup. Two hours later, we went out for dinner and clubbing with her and young Dr. Bellin, alias Captain Crash and the Belly Button Doctor. She looked magnificent, like the cover page of *Vogue*. Huge eyes, beautiful hair, an aristocrat. She was famous and written about in all the magazines.

We got along immediately.

She had two boys—my nephews. Their house on Park Avenue was always filled with the cream of New York. Her parties were legendary. The Who's Who of the world. Bankers, politicians, Jagger, Onassis. The Duke and Duchess's daughter, the Loebs, the Astors. The dinner parties were legendary and eclectic. Her husband, Howard Bellin, was an intern then at Mt. Sinai Hospital. We used to go up to visit them, and she would stay over between his shifts. I couldn't quite understand the relationship, but it appeared to work for them.

He was from New Jersey and Jewish, and I was from Long Island and Jewish. We got along great. No jealousy, no competition. He took a lot of heat and took a punch well. Later, he joined the Air Force and was shipped out to Homestead Air Force Base outside of Miami. He was still in residency to be a plastic surgeon. Howard was a mensch. Whenever there were disasters, he went around the world to do free surgery for the injured.

The two sisters would fight, make up, fight, and make up. Her kids were always at my house when I got home, and my kids were always going over to theirs. She introduced me to everybody. She would say, "This is my brother in law, Bare-bare, isn't he cute? He's married to Franfran, my sister." I heard that hundreds of times. She always looked out for my best interests, but now all the parties are a blur.

I was getting fed up with the East Side real estate business. It was time to be out on my own. I didn't need—or want—to be in business with anybody. Stanley was also unfortunately turning into an alcoholic. Poor Stan. He would come into the office at two after I had already been there since eight in the morning, ask what was going on, lock himself in a small office, and work on the deposit. Business was booming, and checks and cash were coming in every day. He would tally it up, and go out and make the deposit. We usually worked late because stewardesses and pimps wanted to look at places after work. I was there until eight or nine and would always go straight home. He would go down to the local bar and drink. My other partner, Harold, was very sick and in the hospital. He had lung cancer. His job was to secure big buildings outside of Manhattan for us to rent. Stan would take a month off at a time, and I would be left trying to control Rodney Sheldon, Jimmy Hamburger, Maddie Paddy, and a bunch of other damaged hangers-on, all fifteen of them. It was getting old, quickly.

Columbus Avenue and the West Side began to go through a process of gentrification. People were renovating brownstones, and digging gaping holes in the process. I decided to give up the East Side and open up an office on 83rd and Columbus, two blocks from a police station. One block west of my office was like Hell's Kitchen. One block east, and you were on Central Park next to the great old-fashioned high rises of the turn of the century. There was the museum on 81st Street and lots of little cafes. There was Victor's at 72nd and Columbus, and Papaya King at 72nd and Broadway. They shot *Panic in Needle Park* very near my office.

The office on West 83rd was owned by two Eastern European refugees. They both had numbers on their arms. A. Chiness kept his cigar in the corner of his mouth, and always wore his crusty felt hat, and droopy moustache; I called him Abraham.

The building had just been renovated, and we took the first floor duplex, which had two bedrooms and three different entrances. It was perfect. We put in some furniture and opened for business.

Maddie Paddy was in Jack Rosenthal's building, down on 11th Street. Jimmy and Rodney opened up their own place on 51st Street, with Steady Eddie Edelman, the owner—51st between 2nd and 3rd, all furnished apartments. They were friends and buddies, but I'd had enough. I was glad to see them go. Too much drama. I liked the West Side. Goodbye, three-piece suits, goodbye, Chesterfield. Leather jackets, leather pants, boots, shoulder holster, and beads. Let the hair grow.

My doormen started to look at me strangely, but the country was changing, the music was changing, and people were protesting in the streets as the '60s rolled on. Sly and the Family Stone were happening. It was now the land of the Mamas and the Papas.

Maddie called me one day and said a friend of hers needed a job. He was in trouble with the law; he was a good kid from Brooklyn, a little crazy and violent, but he'd cover your back. She thought I could use him. And into my life came Philip Carlo, who is today the author of many books on child abuse, satanic cults, and mafia hit men. Philip came in for an interview. He had shoulder-length hair. He was so good-looking he was pretty. He had on a leather coat with a fur collar, an all-velvet shirt open to his navel, and lots of chains.

"I'm here to be interviewed," he said.

He was intelligent, streetwise, and dangerous. We hit it off immediately. He became my kid brother, protector, and confidant in capers and business. He was from the toughest part of Brooklyn, Bensonhurst, where many of the boys came from. He was a Goodfella, and knew the nightlife. He was a regular at the clubs like Hippopotamus. He started working for me as a salesman, and I got him licensed.

They started to come back again: the pimps, the hookers, the bored Eastsiders who moved to the West Side where the new action was. On one of my first days, a gray-haired guy came in and told me he was the landlord, had ten buildings around the area, and wanted me to run them. We went out to have coffee, and he showed me his .38, which he had a permit for. He gave me a bunch of keys, his supers' names, and said, "Fill 'em up." He added, "Get yourself a gun. You'll need it."

Fill them up we did. Up and down the streets, people were renovating. They needed tenants, and they came by to see me. We put signs up on the buildings, and the people poured in. I knew it was time to buy some buildings on Columbus Avenue, but I had trouble putting money together because my overhead was so high at the house, with the kids and school. It was time for Francesca's mother to help me. I was a good father, I was behaving, and I thought I was a pretty good husband, given the situation.

My dad offered to give me some money if the Contessa would match it. She came up with chump change. I never was able to buy the buildings because I couldn't get the down payment together. Sad for me. I was there at the right time, in the right place, with the right product. I just couldn't deliver. Money was going out faster than it was coming in, and I never seemed to be able to get a big enough lump of cash together.

After that I knew I wasn't going to get any help from the Contessa. She talked a lot about how rich the family was, but she made both sisters crawl for every penny she gave them.

•◊•◊•

Philip moved in near me, on West End Avenue and 71st Street. It was a cozy one-bedroom. It was great to have him close by.

The following summer, I had a nice big house on Fire Island. Philip had the room downstairs, and I had the family upstairs. By now, I had been working with the boys for years. They became friends and buddies.

That summer was the strangest of all. Another man was sent in, a friend of Philip's and Simon's. His name was C. Bradley Mendelssohn. Today, he is vice president of a huge real estate firm. I'm proud of him, but I hope his wife doesn't read this. Bradley had shoulder-length hair and was dressed like Philip, except he was tall and skinny, always with a cigarette in his mouth.

"What are you doing here? What do you want?" I asked.

"I've been in Morocco, wandering around a few years. I need a job."

Evidently, Philip and Bradley had a little bad blood between them. It was a love-hate thing. I said, "Philip, what do you think?"

He said, "Brad can sell anything. Use him."

I was sitting in the office, talking to Bradley, and we got jammed. Philip ran out to show an apartment, and I was the only one left. Just then, a huge Eldorado pulled up, and in walked one of my old pimps, named Bear. As big as a bear, with a fur coat, and two ladies, half-undressed. He said he needed a place immediately.

"I don't have the time right now," I said.

He threw out a pile of hundreds and a vial.

"Bradley, get in Bear's car, take him down there. The apartment's four hundred a month. Get rent and two months' security—get twelve hundred and bring him back. And if you don't get the money, don't come back. Go!"

Two hours later, Bradley walked in. Obviously, he'd been smoking and coking with the Bear. The girls were disheveled, and Bradley threw the cash on the table.

"I gave Bear the keys and a hug," he said. Bear threw me another vial, and thanked me. I gave Bradley a hundred dollar bill. He was hired.

•◊•◊•

Years before the movie *Jaws* came out, Philip and I were out fishing in Montauk and I decided to get some dinner. We went to a restaurant where they had the jaw of a great white shark on the wall. It was ten feet long. You could drive a Volkswagen through it. Right next door was a boat called the *Cricket*. The Captain was named Frank Mundus. He was the Captain in *Jaws* that Robert Shaw played. I learned from some local captains that Peter Benchley got the idea from Montauk—not from Martha's Vineyard.

We were fascinated at the size of the shark's mouth, and tried to charter the *Cricket* to take us out. We met Mundus. He was crusty, obnoxious, and drunk, just like in *Jaws*. We figured out that it would not be a good match. We asked around the bar, and they gave us the name of a younger captain who was cheaper and would do the job. We booked him.

Three weeks later, we arrived at the hotel in Montauk. We had shotguns, bows and arrows, pistols, M4 firecrackers, and dynamite. We were so high that night, I don't think any of us slept. The next morning we had a hardy breakfast, picked up our sandwiches, and met the captain. The boat looked small and old, and I was a bit disappointed. We went out thirty miles on a clear, beautiful July day, and started to fish with big, heavy fishing rods—like in *Jaws*. We bailed blood and chum, and waited, while we caught a number of small bluefish to use as bait.

By nine o'clock we got our first shark. It was a blue. It pulled, it pulled; we fought it and gave it off to each other. It came close to the boat, and we let it go. In the next two hours, we caught two or three more, and I don't know why, but we decided to snort some mescaline. The fourth shark wasn't so lucky. As he came to the edge of the boat, Philip blew a hole in its head. And we tied it around the front of the boat as a trophy. Of course, the water was full of blood, more sharks showed up to eat that shark, and now the fight was on: bows and arrows, shotguns, dynamite in the sharks' mouths, blood, carnage, and hallucinations. Victory at sea.

Finally, we had six sharks tied to the front of the boat, and the captain said we had enough, and we were getting into a dangerous position, as there were sharks all around us. So, one by one, we cut them loose and headed back. We heard a sonic boom, or an explosion somewhere off in the distance. We were very confused as to what it was. Then again, we were tripping. We were high.

About four hundred yards off the starboard bow, the water started to churn and bubble. We could feel the wake against our small vessel. It started to come out of the water. Bigger and bigger, and fierce-looking.

We were a football field away from a nuclear submarine on maneuvers. We weren't sure it was American. We loaded our shotguns and our bows: we were ready for war. The submarine came up—and damned if it wasn't three football fields long and a football field high, at least in my mind—what was left of it that day. I'd never seen one up close, and with the heat lightning we saw on the horizon and the crackling, we thought there was an excellent possibility that the United States was in a nuclear war. We were sure of it. And since we only had our shotguns and rifles and were so high, we felt it was best to cut the sharks loose. Of course, their heads were blown open and they had been chewed up by other sharks. I regret that. That was a big mistake. I should definitely have caught and released. But since I was with three other lunatics, the adrenaline kicked in and we started to shoot, fire, and scream. We got into the collective consciousness of murder. That's the truth, and the mescaline magnified everything.

And I also regret seeing all the bulls weakened and killed with the blood drained from them at the *corridas*. If they didn't weaken the bulls by stabbing them, I could deal with it. I think, more so than not, I'm a macho man, but how cruel. Papa Hemingway, it sucks, it really does. When I mention it, people look at me as if to say, "Where were you, buddy?" Of course, the manners and mores today have changed toward animals. I don't see a lot of fur coats these days, or maybe it's just that I don't get out as much.

When we got back to land, we were still in a high state of thrill-seeking. Philip and Zack Berg, another friend, continued to stab the bluefish we were trying to filet. I have pictures of this, and it's quite sick.

About four months later, Philip, Zack, my dad and I went blue-fishing off Jones Beach, Long Island. My dad was a throwback from Brooklyn—very strong, powerful, virile, and an expert fisherman.

The boat left the harbor, and we cleared the waters off Jones

Beach. As we arrived on the cholera banks, there were fifty other boats out there with lights on—it's quite a sight at night, with the water shimmering. Everybody throws chum in the water, and you hear them all screaming as the rods bend in half.

We started landing fish, one after another. You have to be very careful when you take the hooks out. You can't be too stoned; bluefish teeth can take your fingers off. We weren't that stoned—just some mild reefer madness. After four or five fish, we started getting exhausted. Blood all over the floor, slippery bags full of fish, tangles, screaming, yelling... Zack got tired and sat down. Then Philip and I did, too.

My father landed a large fish and started to pull it over the rail. He swung his rod, and the fish went over the rail, through the window and landed in the lap of the captain—who was fifteen feet up, reading the newspaper and drinking coffee—and started biting him. The captain was stunned at suddenly finding a 20-pound bluefish in his lap. It was a missile, a biting missile. Even with a club beating they won't die. They're like a yellowtail with teeth.

Of course, we made apologies, but these things happen during night fishing.

I quit. My father started laughing at all three of us and called us a bunch of pussies. He kept fishing for another three hours. He was crazed.

About fifty feet away I noticed a boat that I'd seen before, the Victory, and it looked like a charter of cops and firemen. I thought they were cops because several were wearing shoulder holsters, which I thought was really ridiculous when you're out night fishing. They had garbage cans in the middle of the boat filled with bluefish—there was no limit. I really thought the boat was going to sink. They started screaming and yelling and evidently a fight erupted on the boat. I heard "Motherfucker this," "Cocksucker that," "Your aunt is Italian pastrami," and "You no-good Jew bastard," and then shots were fired. I don't think they were really firing at each other, I just think they were letting out their emotions and firing at the black sea. I couldn't quite believe it, but I heard the shots hitting the water and Philip, who is an expert in ballistics and weapons, told me what was going on. He was pissed off because he'd left his guns at home.

I said, "Thank God!"

Three months later the story came out in *Sports Illustrated* Magazine, written by Zack's older brother, who was on the staff. My father was described as "the Samson with the rod." He loved it and showed all his friends.

•◇•◇•

I entered Dr. Freiman's office, rolling up my sleeve, like so many of the super-rich in those days. They called him Dr. Feelgood. He looked in my eyes and, with his German accent, whispered in my ear, "Son, I'm going to make you hotter than you've ever been before," and shot the amphetamine in my arm.

Two days later I was begging Francesca to give me more Secanols so I could sleep. I'd been raging through the village like a madman. Right then, I knew I'd never be that much of a drug addict.

Chapter 9:
Twist and Shout

My mania, my addictions, my need for action dominated all the consciousness I could muster. I may have been living unconsciously in a bad dream, but it was my dream. I was swept up by the times and was sweeping myself into a moral disaster zone. I was in a vortex.

We were dealing in commodities: human flesh and drugs.

Imagine women who are suppressed and put into the lowest rung of society—the whores, hos, stroll workers, receptacles for sperm—rebelling and turning the tables on their keepers—pimps, mac-men, and players in the life. I sat before pimps as a professional and asked them if they were godly enough to take my money. I questioned their credibility, their sensitivity, and their attitudes.

That's exactly what happened to me in New York City, in the early seventies. I controlled the buildings that these people lived in. I had the ultimate power—on all sides of the plate: the women, the men, and—best of all—the money. I was making money by hiring ex-prostitutes and getting them licensed as real estate brokers. They turned out to be great salespeople.

A free spirit came to my door one day, beaten and broken, whining and crying that she couldn't take it anymore. She was going to leap, going to jump, going to shoot.

"Sit down, spend a little time, tell me the story, it can't be that bad."

"It is that bad," she said.

Of her own free will, she gave the money up. Sold her ass for the cheese, and had to return it for the *please*. This young woman from Queens—well-educated, articulate, and intelligent—rebelled against her parents and society by falling in love with a pimp. A street man. Mr. Mac. She was with him for years. She put his father in business, clothed him in leathers and suedes, and supplied him with everything he needed so he could be a peacock.

"What can I do for you?" I asked.

"I need to get away from him," she said.

"Then call the police."

"I can't—he beats me up. He threatens me. I have a certain amount of cash. I need a place to live. I just need a bed. I can make money to keep myself. I just want to get away from him."

What could I do? I took the cash, found a place, and put her in it. I didn't hear anything for a month or two, she paid the rent, and then the call came. Somebody was breaking up an apartment, ranting and raving, beating someone else. The super called me. I called her, told her that this no longer could continue. I said, "It has to be dealt with on my end or your end. My end is to get you out for breaking your lease. And your end is to get him out, so you can stay. There is no middle."

One day six months later, she came in looking like a new person, with new clothes, all dressed up. She brought me a present.

"How nice, but what do you want me to do with the five-eight beauty sitting next to you?"

"That's a gift for you," she said.

"Thank you for the offer, I'll take a rain check."

"This is my friend. She's leaving her man just like I did, and she needs a place. She's got a certain amount of cash. She needs a bed."

Same deal. I took the money and three months later got a call. Again, somebody there, breaking down the door in the middle of the night. I made the call, but didn't hear anything. A couple of months later, she came in with another girl, same story, same program, same results—except I did not get a call on this apartment. Three different buildings, three different women.

They were doing very well, and I suggested that they bring some others in.

They went into business. They got johns to give them cash to get furnished apartments, and rented them out to pimps to get the overage. It got out of control, and it was drawing me in. But it was fascinating. Why would somebody give their money up to somebody else just to make them feel lower?

Then came Sly. He arrived at my doorstep telling me that he knew people I knew; he heard that I had great apartments, and that his skin color and his occupation didn't matter. He needed an apartment.

"I'm not sure. I have certain buildings, and I have a code, and you have to pay a lot of money for a place in one of my buildings."

I took his money, gave him the rules and the regs, and put him in another building in not such a good area—where he could shine. This procedure exploded. Two, three, or four a week showed up at my office needing housing. I could find vacancies, the market was soft, and they needed to rent.

I made it clear it was for living and not for tricking; trick pads were different. I had them in other buildings. These were family buildings. It got out of control. They were lined up in their "hogs"—these pimp-mobiles—in front of my office, night and day, waiting in my areas in their costumes, pouring through my doors, going all over Manhattan. Soon, I had no more room for them.

That's when I met Fast Black.

One afternoon, I was sitting in my office. In walks D'Artagnan, the true Third Musketeer. He's dressed all in black, with a plumed hat, tight black leather pants, a tight black leather jacket, and a black scarf—a handsome devil.

"My name is Fast Black. I figures it's time to come see you 'cause you're takin' all the money from my ladies!"

"Yes, Mr. Fast, I'm taking all the money."

Of course, on my left I have a shotgun against the wall. It was the Wild West in New York City.

"Yes, Fast Black," I added, "your reputation precedes you."

"Motherfucker," he said, "talk English."

"First rule," I said, "I'm not the motherfucker. Maybe you're the motherfucker. I get the respect now!"

"I'm sorry, I'm sorry, I'm sorry," he said.

"What do you want?"

"I want a big place," he said, "one of those duplexes. I got a group comin' in from Nashville, two fine white ladies."

"Well, Fast, I'll get one of the girls to take you out."

"I don't want some ho. I want you."

"Black, I don't do that right now."

He put a pile on the table, which I couldn't get into my pocket. He put two vials of coke down, put some smoke down, and he said, "Let's go for a ride. I got my new hog."

I looked outside. All black chrome, leg plugs—it looked like Clarabelle the Clown's car.

"I think I'll take my Cadillac. I don't wanna take that thing," I said. "It looks like it might have some diseases in it."

Then I looked at my watch. It was three and I'd missed lunch.

"Alright," I said, "I'll let you take me to get something to eat."

Fast Black and I got into his car. I slid down into the seat. Barry White is going "Deeper and Deeper." Fast broke open a vial and flipped it my way, and we started to get to know each other.

He says, "Lemme stop by, I wanna introduce you."

Well, a red light went off, but I figured, "Ah, I'm a god tonight anyway." We went down to University Place. I had a building there renovated by two Holocaust refugees—wood-burning fireplace, high ceilings, spiral staircase, Jacuzzi—it was beautiful.

Being dyslexic, I had always found it challenging to take people around and show them apartments because the numbers on the floor plans all looked backwards to me. So in my spare time, I had memorized the stacks of floor plans of all the buildings I managed, until I had no problem escorting people around. I can still remember them all now, unfortunately. This was one of my advanced coping mechanisms that had its drawbacks.

Fast stopped off at his hotel, came down with two skinny tens and put them in the hog. We were all bobbin' and weavin', soakin' and smokin'. We went down to the pad, and he loved it. Then he took me over to the West Side near 10th Avenue for lunch in a big back room. It was ribs, chicken, and candied yams. We ate and laughed all night long. Fast and I became tight after that. Any problems out on the street, Fast knew what to do. He was Fast Black.

I often spent Saturday nights in a two-bedroom apartment with fifteen pimps and twenty girls watching the Knickerbockers. I was the only white person in the place, among the screaming kids and pots cooking with food—ribs and chicken.

One evening I was in a fancy restaurant with my wife and my friends, and there were groups of people who looked like circus clowns, drinking champagne, making noise, and throwing hundred dollar bills around. Several of them spotted me and shouted, "It's him! It's my man Barry!" They came over to my table with their boobs hanging out, and mini mini-skirts, tattoos (before it was fashionable) and brought me bottles of champagne, saying, "Compliments of your friends!" I was there with doctors, lawyers, politicians, and my mother-in-law, the Contessa.

I stopped going out to restaurants with my family and friends.

I sat back on my sofa at about nine-thirty one night with a pile of cash and a few lines of coke, and tried to understand why somebody would give all their money and possessions away to be beaten, kicked, humiliated, and destroyed. I understood the concept of low self-worth and coming from nothing and not having a daddy or a mommy, but it was still too confusing for me. I became fixated on this question. The deeper I thought about it, the more I realized the only way to really find out about it was to live it.

The money I got made me feel like one of them. I could take the money, but I didn't have the consciousness to inflict the pain and torture they did. But it was boring a hole in my consciousness. I had to figure it out, by doing it.

I went about gathering my stable. One deep. Two deep. Three deep. Four deep. Five deep. There were ex-prostitutes, who were now licensed real estate brokers, working for me. As I was doing my research, I didn't get addicted to the drugs. I was chipping. I got addicted to the sex. After a while, the sex didn't work—as with drugs, you reach a point where it doesn't get you that high anymore. The sex stopped doing anything for me. I needed more, and different. I needed something, like a crutch. I didn't realize it at the time, but I was bipolar and manic depressive.

Things slipped out of control, and I illegally got a .38 Smith and Wesson, with an extra-long barrel, and kept it in my drawer, loaded. I also had my trusty shotgun, fully visible, which was there for show. The word on the street was that some people we were involved with were robbed at gunpoint, and the same perpetrators were talking about an office on 83rd and Columbus, which had drawers of cash and high-grade cocaine. I dismissed the rumor as a lot of talk. The truth was, we didn't have that much cash, and there was *never* much cocaine, just a few ounces at a time, and the cash was chump change in those days. We mostly did it to show off.

But I had the gun in the drawer, just in case. Could I use it? If somebody came in, could I cold-bloodedly shoot them if they menaced me or it looked like I was going to be ripped off? It's an interesting question. To take a human life, to blow a hole in the chest of someone you don't know, under the assumption that they're going to do it to you first? The gun was there. I loaded and reloaded it, and cleaned it, thought about it, fixated on it, and I believe that if somebody came in and threatened my life, that I could have used it—and I wouldn't have hesitated.

But, looking back now at that room and that situation, I'm not so sure I would have pulled the trigger. They never came. I never used the gun, but I was sinking quickly—just the thought was chilling, to be put in that position, with three children at home, this other life, with private schools and respectability. As Brando's character said in *Apocalypse Now*, "The snail that's crawling on the razor is having a hard time."

I sat back and said to myself, *Here I am, five or six years after being jailed for smuggling, and I'm doing the same thing, when I promised I wouldn't. What's the matter with me? Why am I drawn to this life?* Was I an action junkie? Or a past-life reincarnation of somebody? Was it karma? I'm not sure, but I know I was having a good time.

•◇•◇•

Going out every night and carrying a gun was bad for my relationship at home. But I made sure I put the boys to sleep first. One day a week, we would go to the movies, and often to 42nd Street near Broadway to the opening of a new one. Other nights I'd be out alone in clubs or at fancy parties. Francesca had returned to her love of reading and didn't care about going out that much. At that point in my life, all I cared about was money and action, and books meant nothing to me. I was a fool.

Meanwhile, at the real estate office, life was getting more desperate. The pimps' cars were double-parked. They recognized me all over town.

Life was getting more complicated. I got a call from one of my Cuban rental connections. A friend of theirs was coming into town and needed a place to live. I met Carlos at 83rd and Columbus in a coffee shop. He had a scar down the left side of his face, and a hole in his palm like somebody shot through it with a small-caliber pistol.

We visited over coffee, and he told me he needed a brownstone off Central Park West for living, with no doorman. I had an apartment for him at a thousand a month. I needed rent and two months security. We walked around the corner, and I opened the door. He walked in and out, and gave me three crisp thousand-dollar bills. I was a little apprehensive because it was my first experience with thousands. Usually, it was hundreds. I thanked him, and told him I'd have the keys in a couple of days. He said, "Fine." I walked over to Chemical Bank, and they said they were real. I folded them up and put them into my wallet.

A week later, Carlos called. He said he needed a second apartment for his girlfriend. We met at the coffee shop. Same transaction—walked in, walked out, three more thousand-dollar bills. I had keys for him, and told him he was my new best friend. This was around January, right after New Year's.

•◇•◇•

Francesca and I decided that we would spend the next summer on Fire Island. We had friends down the block whose kids were in the same class with our kids—nice people. We went out there and found a scenic house a half-block from town. I paid out those three thousand-dollar bills. The real estate broker gave me the stink eye as he stuffed them into his wallet.

Memorial Day weekend. Moving Day. Maids, mother's helpers, and other couples moved out to Fire Island. The first night we were there, Francesca got into a screaming fight with Vivian, one of the neighbors, about the house and the rooms. These were cheap little houses, and it was raining so hard, one of the bedroom walls caved in. I was told it was time to move, so after one night and three thousand dollars I had to go out and spend more money. The next day, we moved up the block, to another house, at the same price, fifteen hundred a month. That was the end of my beautiful thousand-dollar bills. Easy come, easy go, but it wasn't so easy come—for me. I was putting my neck out.

That was the summer of the seaplane. Friday afternoon, from 28th Street, I'd take the seaplane to Fire Island, jump out and wade in. An hour later, after I got settled, she would get on her seaplane and be off for the weekend. Flying seaplanes.

By now, I was deeply involved with "the boys." I was filling up their buildings and getting compensated.

I had to take a trip down to Puerto Rico to do some business, and I took a couple of builders with me. We were sitting by the pool, and an attractive woman with a European accent came up to me.

"My name is Xaviera."

"What a nice name. What are you doing down here?"

"Oh, I'm on holiday, just getting some sun. Do you mind if I sit down?"

"No," I said. "It's a free world, put it there."

The other guys I was with were smoking cigars and playing gin rummy, so I visited with her. She said she was in the Life, and asked if I would like some action? I told her the last thing I needed was action or to talk to anyone in the Life. I was trying to escape it. I was there on business. She asked me if I was staying there, and told me she was having a little trouble with the hotel. Could she change to our suite and have some dinner? I said sure, come on up.

The next day we chartered a boat and planned to do some fishing. She asked to come along. I said, "I don't see why not.

Come out and get a suntan."

We were in the middle of the ocean, trolling back and forth. She decided she needed to sunbathe a little more, removing her bathing suit. The captain and the mate stared so hard that the boat went in a circle. Her name was Xaviera Hollander. Later we worked together. I got her some moneymaking residences. She became famous as the Happy Hooker, and she was the most famous madam in New York.

I started to float. I lived in my office on 81st and Park, which was decorated with Pakistani wedding tents and glass tables and lots of plants. In the back room I had a TV, a refrigerator, and a big bed.

The boys got me a nice little apartment on 63rd between Madison and Park with a fireplace and a terrace, a gift for fifty a month. It was an unusual studio. I built a huge loft on top of it for my boys when they came on the weekends.

A woman named Ginger introduced me to swinging, and the Botany Club. From then on, I was *so* out of control! She was bisexual, and her favorite pastime was to bring girls home for *us*. I taught her the real estate business so she could get up during the day and make some money. I couldn't get up since I'd just gotten to sleep. This would go on all week long until my boys came, and then I straightened up and played daddy. Ginger took me around to the gay bars to meet all her girlfriends. The Magnificent Mattress and Cherry Grove, Fire Island.... The underground world of lesbian sex. Ginger managed a place called the Pleasure Chest that sold exotic erotica paraphernalia.

I had so many keys to so many empty apartments that I would float around for days before I'd come home. I also knew many people in all my buildings because I'd put them in. There was always a hot meal and a warm bed.

Chapter 10:
Cheap Perfume

321 East 48th Street was around the corner from my office, where we had a lot of rental apartments. I came up with a plan with Maddie Paddy and Carol, whose boyfriend had a lot of money, and wanted to put them in business. We furnished the apartments, two big ones, and used that as a floating hotel. At 301 East 47th lived Jimmy Hamburger, who was working for me at the time, and his handsome Lab, Alfie. On 49th Street, up in a wraparound penthouse, was Rodney Sheldon. We had the area covered with mental illness, debauchery, narcotics, prostitution, gambling, and extortion.

The 48th Street building was loaded with stewardesses—everyone called them *"stewardii."* Some apartments had six to eight *stewardii.* The lobby of the building looked like JFK before a flight—all the *stewardii* from different airlines with suitcases.

Unfortunately, mingled with the *stewardii* were *pimp-ii.* And some low-level gangsters, money runners for loansharks, baby hitmen. Many buildings on the East Side had that clientele.

One day, the cover story in *New York Magazine* was "Who Did This to New York City?" I wasn't the only one doing it—many followed, after they saw the formula: put people who were considered undesirable in luxury buildings and others would move out—and then you could raise the rents. There were just too many apartments in New York—and too many ruthless landlords and rental agents. People were taking their children out in baby carriages as pimps pulled up in cars, unloading their "hos." It didn't work.

I never really felt a hostile attitude from any of the pimps when they came in to get the apartments. Maybe I should have, but I didn't. It seemed natural that they should be giving their money to ex-hookers, to give me money to accommodate them with buildings that they couldn't get on their own. To me, it was just business. There was nothing personal about the transfer of currency, and those "hos" sure knew how to count hundred dollar bills.

It was strange that a licensed real estate saleswoman, a former "ho," took money from a mac-man with one of his "hos" sitting next to him, while he was telling everybody how great he was, as he was turning over money to get his keys.

And then I would send out Maddie Paddy or Trish or one of the other girls with these pimps to look at apartments. I always asked, "Did you have any problems?" And they said, "No, they were perfect gentlemen. They never tried to pull me, and they always gave us some good blow in the car—and a joint when we went into the apartments to look at them." After all, it was the '70s.

The only problem occurred when these guys would slap their women around and make a lot of noise, and the neighbors complained that they heard banging on the walls—which was the girls' heads. Some of the pimps did terrible things. They'd put a wire hanger in a towel and whip the women on their backs and all over their legs. It didn't "damage the merchandise." They just whipped away at them. There was an occasional black-eye, loose tooth or purple lip covered with makeup. I saw it all. I didn't say much because I was counting out the cash. Nothing personal. Just business.

I used to ask the girls why they let these guys do that to them, and they'd just say, "He's just showin' he cares." Any reaction, whether good or bad, was better than no reaction.

Why I couldn't see the terrible darkness in all this troubles my conscience still. I was a clown, a freak, and even the most ridiculous behavior somehow passed by me without a wince. I now know how limited my self-awareness was, and I watched a world exist that now would drive me crazy. I hate abuse, violence, the maltreatment of human beings. But there I was, in the middle of a moral nowhere zone, hammering the nails in my own coffin, staying stoned. There were no ethics, no boundaries. There was no intuitive knowledge of just how far down I was going. It was a nightmare that I awoke to day after day. They would come and go and bring their friends and their friends' friends. Slowly I became so curious about what they did in my office that I wanted to know what they did at night. I asked them where they ate, what they did for recreation, and where they went. Most of them had their main house, which was just for living, cooking, maybe some stash—clothes that they boosted, furs, some jewels, and anything they could turn for dollars. But no tricking was done there.

Most of the girls worked on the stroll, or some who had *trick books* worked in their own apartments. And the pimp would come around and collect at the end of the day, or every couple of days. If he couldn't make it, he would send his main woman or top lady, the girl that he trusted the most, and had been with him the longest. She would go out and check his traps and pull in the line. And lord help the ho who tried to cheat. There would be pain to pay.

I would see them in Madison Square Garden at a Knicks game in the best seats, wearing their furs and their finest, or ringside at a big fight. Some nights, when I was working late, the pimps would invite me to Small's for some ribs and chicken. Or down at the Boondocks on 11th and the River. It was great. We would talk about sports, business, children, and home. Many were from Florida, and most were from big cities in the South: Nashville, Memphis, Savannah, St. Louis. They ran from the age of twenty-one chicken pimps, to old poppas in their forties. They had names, from "Fast Black" to "Dog" to "Sheep" to "Goat" to "Pinky." There was Benny T., R.R., B.R., J.R., Doody-R. They had watches, rings, chains, diamonds, coats to match hats, boots to match belts. It was like a circus.

We got around to talking about basketball, and they'd invite me back to their home pads to watch the Knicks games. I sat around with ten black men in their underwear, with boots, hats, chains, and watches, doing toot, eating ribs and chicken, drinking whiskey, yelling, and talking about the game.

Then I would stagger home in the middle of the night, sleep for a few hours, tend to the kids, change my clothes, check on my guns, put my cash away, and go back to work.

This was my way of life.

Then the rush started. The cars lined up, the money flowed, and the dope sold. I became so busy that the girls who worked for them started to work for me.

Of course, on nights out, I also had my social obligations: Park Avenue parties with senators, congressmen, models, actors, actresses, and great writers. With my three-piece suits and Brooks Brothers coats, I felt like Superman—or Clark Kent, depending on the night.

Unfortunately, I started to get confused. I'd be wearing my leathers and my suedes and my silks when I should have been wearing my Brooks Brothers suit. In the middle of a conversation about Machiavelli, I would start to talk about candied yams, beans, rice, and wire coat hangers. I have to say, people listened. People wanted to sit next to me at dinner parties and come over to my group. I'd be quoting Voltaire, and next, I'd be telling them how much a gram cost on the street that night.

And then I had to check on the girls who worked for me in real estate during the day, making sure they stayed out of trouble, because most of them had money from the previous night, when they went out to show the apartments.

I kept my pocket money in my boots so I wouldn't be robbed, but I was starting to get calluses and cuts from the lumps. And I often dropped a little automatic pistol from my waist. It would fall on the floor at the wrong times.

I got so obsessed that I decided to make a movie about all this. I found a cameraman, a would-be actress who was one of my tenants, an assistant director, and we went out and shot it. I still have it.

I tried to buy Iceberg Slim's book, *Trick Baby*, but it didn't work out. The next thing I knew, *Superfly* was out, as well as *Shaft*, and a bunch of other black movies, and they were raking in the cash.

I came home stinking of cheap perfume from the guys and

the girls. My wife would wet down my side of the bed, and when I got home, my sheets were ice cold.

Things were not working out.

Most of the people I'm writing about who were in the Life are dead, I am sure. The big pimp daddies? I think they're gone. A few may be in their 70s—God bless them.

Ginger and I walked down Madison Avenue, and whether we went into a bar or a restaurant, or sat in the park, we would find a player for the evening. Often they would seek us out—or seek her or me out. Most of the players were women.

The attraction was always to the feminine side. It usually wound up that we would find a woman who never had a lesbian experience before, though she had thought about it but never wanted to go through with it. This discussion would usually happen before we got back to our house.

Once back in the playpen, the drugs, the paraphernalia, the fireplace, the massages and the baths were all available to bring us all together. It almost always worked, and it was magnetic. Or, if I picked up a girl and brought her home, sometime during the evening we would be in a ménage.

And it wasn't just with Ginger, but with other girls that I went out with, and they could be straight—or not. I asked them to help me—and they did. I think it was the times, and people were curious—everybody was experimenting, and I don't just mean the people from the Botany Club or Plato's Retreat. I'm talking about the Long Island housewives, the secretaries, and the next-door neighbors.

In my world, everybody was jumping into the pond.

One day, on East 74th Street in one of our offices, Philip was throwing his knife against the wall, Zack was talking on the phone, and an attractive woman came in to fill out an application for one of our apartments. I was sitting there talking to her. I must have been very high, and she picked up a contact high, but I asked her if she'd mind if I unbuttoned her blouse. Instead of slapping me, she let me open her blouse. She was bra-less. As I was fondling her breasts, Philip grew interested and put his knife away, and Zack put the phone down. I sensed immediate danger with these two freaks, and I thanked her, took her rent and security, and told her to button up her blouse. Why did she let me do that, though? I still don't understand.

On another afternoon, Philip, Zack, Bradley, and I were all sitting in the office, doing our usual subleasing routine. Bradley started talking back to Philip, and the next thing I knew, Bradley was hanging out of the window by his heels. I did my best to persuade Philip not to drop him. It wasn't a good idea—right across the street was a building controlled by the boys, and our job was security, keeping things under control.

Bradley still ended up with bright red scratches on his head, but I felt he'd deserved it.

The landlady barged in, shrieking, "What's all this noise? You guys gotta shut up!"

Philip calmly replied, "I'm terribly sorry." He then pulled out his cigarette lighter and lit the drapes on fire. The woman tripped and fell down on the floor, peed on herself, and departed hastily, shaking.

We had to move after that. Somebody had seen Bradley hanging out the window and called the police. It was quite an afternoon.

I was working hard most of the time, and we were making money in spite of our antics. On another occasion, two Swedish women were sent over from one of our other buildings to sign a lease to rent an apartment. Zack and I were alone that day. The young ladies started giving us a hard time; they didn't want to sign this paper or that paper. Zack was so high that he fell out of his chair laughing and crumpled on the floor in front of them. I picked up my chair, broke it in half, and threw it against the wall. Zack picked up another chair and smashed it against the wall. Our furniture was antiques from one of the stores that we had ripped off because it had been dispossessed, and we proceeded to smash all of it in front of these two women. They didn't move, they just sat still for a while, until the room looked like a bomb had gone off. Then they signed the papers and left. We laughed uproariously, then realized it was time to take another lude and another hit. Another afternoon at the office.

In the beginning, I felt I was on a mission to act like this, but I lost control. Naturally, I was paying the police to allow all the double parking and had the perimeters protected by the wise guys. But I was trying to save as many of the women as possible. And I had developed compassion in jail. The irony was that in spite of my good intentions, it was my sexual addiction that got me close to them. But I listened to their stories, and I learned about poverty and a woman's perspective.

One of the girls, whom I'll call Cindy, was from Westchester. Her father was a successful dentist. She told me that when she was younger, he used to creep into her bed and fondle her, tell her sexual stories, masturbate while he was talking to her, and make her hold him. Her mother caught them and blamed her rather than him. By the time she was sixteen, she was having sex with the postman, one of the delivery boys at the local hardware store, and the man who owned the local grocery store. At seventeen, she moved into the city, and there she met her pimp. She told me that he was kind and gentle in the beginning. He took her shopping, told her she was an angel, took her out to fancy restaurants, and bought her presents. He didn't ask her to turn any tricks in the beginning, and said, "Baby, do me a favor. Go see this guy, go see that guy." She worked out of a trick book that his top lady, or main woman, had. Within a year, she was doing heroin. He kept her supplied—and stoned half the time.

Finally, he was stabbed and killed by another pimp, and she was able to escape, set up her own business and was very successful.

Many of them transferred their emotions towards me by telling me their stories. But what could I do to help them? The truth is, I couldn't. I could share sex with them, and not be a john. I could be a friend. And they did not have to be hookers. They were not compensated in any way, except emotionally— which is not what they do. I was honestly trying to help them and, perhaps, rationalizing that I could. I did succeed in giving them real work, but it was probably naïve of me to think I had the necessary skills to help them in the long term.

Quite a few broke down in tears, though, and said they hadn't cried in years. I have to admit, I was a good listener, and a few times I welled up with them and hugged them. When they became my employees, it was very difficult, because I was their father figure, even though we were the same age and I was their boss, and they loved giving me the cash. They'd say, "Here, Daddy, here's the money." I had sponsored them and they were now licensed real estate brokers, so when they rented apartments I gave them their commissions, which they were not used to, so they could pay their rents and their living expenses, and not have to go back on the stroll. I thought my approach was somewhat redeeming because once they were licensed, they were free to work for others as well, so it was long-term help for some, if they continued down that path.

Some made it, like Maddie, Cindy, and Trish. Maddie became a social worker; she remarried and had two children. Cindy opened an advertising agency in another city.   Trish married a builder. I saw others in later years on street corners or in restaurants, looking sallow and drained, still in the Life. I couldn't approach them, it was too painful, as it is even now, thinking and writing about it. But if I saved even a few, I believe I accomplished something meaningful.

One of the girls gave me a key to an apartment for my birthday. This young girl was attached to me emotionally, as close as she could be. I believed she would take a bullet for me. So I got the address and went over there. The door opened, and there was an exquisite-looking Eurasian woman in lingerie, with a ribbon around her, singing "Happy Birthday."

I emerged three hours later, wobbling back to the office, and the girls had a cake for me and sang Happy Birthday. I call that unconditional love, to do that and not be jealous or judgmental. I couldn't even do that for somebody I cared about.

People were getting lost: the Maddie Paddys, the Gingers, hookers I knew who got thrown off terraces because they overheard a conversation, and I was spiraling down. I looked down the barrel of a gun two times in one week through a web of shadows and vague discontent, and it changed everything.

One afternoon, I rang the doorbell of a renovated brownstone. A Southern-accented girl's voice asked, "Who is it?"

"The landlord." I was buzzed in. I found large rooms with high ceilings, and a small bedroom in the back. A beautiful, young blonde girl appeared and said hello, smiling. I don't think I'd ever seen her before.

The pimp yelled from the bedroom, "I'll be right out!" He was two months behind in the rent, and I'd given him too much time already. It was time to collect, and I'd sent someone around the day before to let him know I'd be by to pick up the cash. The room was still dark from the night before, a lamp was lit on the table, and the rest of the place was cheaply furnished with rental furniture. He came out wearing crushed velvet slacks, black boots, and a Stanley Kowalski undershirt. I didn't see the .357 Magnum in his left hand, hanging from his long black fingers. I should have known better.

I was sitting down at the table talking to the girl. He took his other hand, patted me on the back, threw a pile of cash on the table.

"We cool?" I said.

"We're cool!" he said. "Now I'm gonna tell you what I'm gonna do. I can play God."

"I bet you're good at it," I said.

"Watch your mouth, white boy, you're talkin' to God." The hair rose on the back of my neck.

He grabbed my throat in a quick thrust and, in the same motion, pulled the gun up and put it to my temple. The girl screamed and shouted, "What are you doing? What are you doing?" He spat in her face and told her to get out of there, kicking her in the stomach.

"Your daddy can do anything he wants! He's a god and he'll show you what a god he is. He can blow away this white boy right now."

It was hard to breathe. He released his fingers a little and went on to tell me how important he was for the next half hour. She was sniveling in the corner. Another girl came out of the bedroom half-naked and wobbly. Finally, he started to get tired. Obviously, he needed another hit of coke. He let go of my neck and said that he was just fooling.

I scooped the money up, walked outside, sat down on the stoop, and kissed the ground.

The next day, we had an empty apartment. The painters were there, painting it up.

•◇•◇•

Three days later, the veteran walked into my East Side office.

We were in an older World War II building off Park Avenue, and I was sitting in the back with two associates, Ivan the Terrible and Zack Berg, and my redheaded date, Susan.

Normally, we closed at six-thirty in the evening, and I'd usually locked the door by then. I kept it open during the daytime so the clients could come in and out, and since we controlled the building, this was no problem.

I saw him first. I was sitting, facing the open office door. As soon as I saw the door opening, and the man coming in, I knew it was wrong, and the vibe was wrong. He had dark, straggly hair with streaks of gray running through it, a scraggly beard, bad skin, and sad but piercing blue eyes. He wore an army fatigue jacket, a knitted hat over his ears, very creased rolled-up dirty jeans, and combat boots.

He was holding a .32 Beretta.

Ivan was in his sheik's whites, full robes and turban, and Zack and I were in our hippie outfits. Susan was in a conservative office outfit. The man pulled up one of the chairs next to the desk and sat down, and he made us listen to him. He was sweating and shaking, his speech was altered. He smelled of alcohol and living on the streets.

He told us to take off all of our jewelry and put it, and all of our money, on the table. He said nobody listened to him, and we would have to listen before it was over. We didn't know what "over" meant, so we listened.

The phones rang, and somebody was dancing in the apartment above and playing the piano. There was a flash of light outside and a crack of thunder.

He opened our pocketbooks and emptied them. He took our watches and rings and put them on the table. He took a joint from Zack and lit it. We sat there looking at him while he smoked.

He continued to rant. He said that he'd been in Vietnam, and had been forced to kill women and children, and burn villages. He said the government did it to him, and that he'd gotten addicted to heroin. Every day was hell, and now he couldn't sleep because his dreams were so horrible. How could anybody expect him to live?

He went on and on about everything that was wrong. I tried to calm him down. I had four hundred dollars on me, which I gave him.

He didn't calm down, and he told us we were weirdoes who hadn't fought for our country. He told Ivan to face the wall because he was too ugly to live and that he might have to kill him. Ivan turned toward the wall.

Meanwhile, the intercom phone kept ringing, and Zack kept answering it, talking with people about apartments, as the veteran waved his gun at us, chuckling, and continuing to smoke his joint.

I asked him why he didn't lock the door, and what he would do if someone walked in.

"I'll take care of them, too," he said.

I asked him again to lock the door. "My brother-in-law's a doctor, we'll get you what you need," I said.

Susan was wide-eyed. She began to cry, and said, very softly, "Please don't kill me. I have kids. Listen, you said you killed kids over there. Please don't kill me. Please don't kill my kids...."

Zack was still answering the phone as if nothing was going on. Meanwhile, Ivan was standing there in his white pajamas looking at the wall, and Susan was frozen with fear.

Finally, the veteran put most of the money and jewelry back on the table.

"I don't need all this," he declared. "I just need enough to buy heroin."

He apologized, and with tears in his eyes, he said he was sorry that he had troubled us, and wished us all the best of luck. He handed back all of our jewelry and our watches, and told us if he straightened himself out, he'd bring the rest of the money back.

"I'm going to back out of here," he said. "Don't move for five minutes."

He left as silently as he came.

We all staggered around the corner to Willy's Bar on 81st and 3rd. I sat, almost missing the chair. We had a few stiff drinks. Susan was shaking and couldn't quite talk. I had been deathly afraid that she would scream and the vet would overreact, but it hadn't happened.

The next day, I told Francesca I couldn't do it anymore. I was one bullet away from death. I said we should sell this massive apartment and move to Greenwich, the Hamptons, anywhere. We could commute. But I had to get out. Too many guns, too many drugs, racing through too many red lights.

"No, the kids are going to school here, my friends are here, my sister's here, my mother's here, my life is here."

"Could you think about it?" I asked. "I can't be put in this position again."

We had scheduled a trip to St. Thomas. We went as if nothing had happened, and I tried to bring up the subject again. When we got back, we had words. And that was the end of our marriage. The Contessa intervened, and the lawyers showed up.

Chapter 11:

The Botany Club

Sex is the strongest addiction in the world, and I, most certainly, was an addict. Once I tasted it, I was hooked. You might think you weren't, but you'd lie there at night in your own sweat waiting for the next one, waiting for Friday night, and the next show.

Many of us Botany Club members thought about it all week long. We couldn't wait to get to the partying. We kept in touch during the week: Who're you bringing Friday? Who's going to have the best party? Sometimes we'd cheat and have a swing on a Wednesday when we couldn't wait for the weekend.

I took my friend Pete to the Botany Club. Pete was an art dealer from Madison Avenue, a man with good manners, imposing at six-two, and a better-looking Frank Sinatra. His girlfriend was in London for a few weeks.

"Pete, what are you doing over the weekend?" I asked.

"Nothing," he said.

"Would you like to have dinner with me and go over to a club?"

"What kind of club?" he asked.

"Trust me," I said.

Forty-eight hours later, we arrived at a gorgeous triplex in Sutton Place where there was debauchery night and day. I took Pete home. He called me up the following Monday morning and told me that he had gone blind. We called a specialist, and it took him a week to get some of his sight back. He never fully recovered, though. Sorry, Pete. May he rest in peace.

"Stern apartment," I told the concierge.

I got in the elevator with a beautiful young couple, Gene and Carol, who I recognized from another party. We nodded politely to each other.

"Do you know the Sterns well?" Gene asked.

"I think I do, but I'm not sure."

Another couple entered the elevator on the third floor.

"We're going up," I said.

"So are we," the woman answered, "we're going to the Sterns."

Everyone looked around, smiling, imagining what everyone else looked like undressed.

"Okay, great," Gene said to Carol, "you want to stay together or you want to split up?"

"Ah, let's stay together this week. It was exhausting alone last time. I couldn't find you, and then, when I did, we had to leave."

A swing was in progress in this duplex in the exclusive United Nations Plaza Building. The top floor consisted of two adjoining apartments. I looked out the window and saw ships going by, the traffic on FDR Drive, and heard the wail of sirens going to Belleview Hospital. A few helicopters were landing on the PanAm building around the corner. I was swept in with the group from the elevator.

Old Mr. Stern sat in the corner, in his bathrobe, reading the *Wall Street Journal* and checking the stocks as he smoked a joint, disregarding all the chaos around him, while his wife— "the woofer"—crawled around barking like a dog and chasing people's heels. This party had only ten couples. A Liberace look-alike played the piano. Three people lounged in a bathtub-jacuzzi in one room. Everyone was moving very slowly; nobody was in a rush. Some people were dressed, some were in bathrobes and slippers supplied by the host.

Many people went to the Botany Club for punishment as well as pleasure. Men who had been caught in adultery, lies, schemes—their wives brought them there to humiliate them, by making their husbands watch them having sex with other men, while they couldn't do anything except masturbate. Others crawled around the floor in a collar on a leash, barking. And there were the women who had to watch their husbands have sex with other women, or even sit in little girl outfits and get spanked by other girls as punishment for their indiscretions. I walked into a separate room where an older gentleman sat on the floor in a white jacket and diapers. His wife, Marlene, and another couple were embracing and crawling all over each other on the bed.

"Hello," I said.

Dr. Kirk took his bottle out of his mouth. "Good evening," he said.

I read the doctor's name off the name tag on the jacket. "Dr. Kirk. How are you? Are you making house calls, or is this a hospital? What seems to be your problem?"

"I was responsible for taking care of my children on the weekends," he said. "One Sunday afternoon the maid was off, and I had the two small children to take care of. Instead of watching the kids, I got a blow job in the cabana by the pool in my house in Jersey. Both children drowned. So at the Botany Club, I am forced to wear diapers and clothespins on my nipples and suck on a bottle. That's my job every Friday night. I have to watch my wife, Marlene, have sex with women and men, and I'm not allowed to do anything but suck on this bottle."

Finished with her sexual encounter, Marlene walked past me and slapped Dr. Kirk hard in the face, then gave him a cookie.

"Marlene, no treats for Barry?" I asked.

She looked at me. "I have to slap you first."

"Dear lady," I replied, "that's my job. Could I slap you?"

"Oh, you're so boring."

She walked away.

I turned back to Dr. Kirk. "It's a shame you're such a bad boy, doctor."

"Well, I deserve it," he replied. "I'm in hell and purgatory. You can imagine my living conditions. She literally built me a doghouse and feeds me out of a bowl like a dog."

"Dr. Kirk, this must be true. Nobody would make up anything like that."

I roamed. People were sniffing cocaine, taking disco biscuits, and smoking joints. There were pantomimes. People were telling stories and having business discussions. I went over to the bartender, who was one of the half-naked guests.

"Champagne, please."

The bartender nodded and poured it for me.

Nearby, Dean was approached by Margaret, a dazzling blonde.

"Oh, Loverboy!" she said. "Come on into the bedroom!"

Dean indicated his lovely partner, Paula, a few paces away.

"You gotta let her in if you want me," he said. "We're together."

The bartender handed me my drink.

Margaret sighed. "Okay, well, bring 'er! So, do you need a shower? Would you like a bath?"

I spotted Gene and Carol from the elevator and approached them, sipping champagne. They were administering "his and hers" Quaaludes to each other. Like me, they were among the few people in the room who still had their clothes on.

"You don't seem to be having a good time," I remarked to Gene.

"Actually we're having a wonderful time. We're not high enough to join in yet, but we're happy to watch. You know, we're big watchers."

"Oh, I do remember, you're very good watchers. Did the Doctor give you a cookie?"

Gene rolled his eyes. "I feel the Doctor should be put out of his misery, don't you, Barry?"

"Don't be silly, he enjoys every minute of it."

"You think so?" Carol asked me, fascinated.

"Absolutely. He's like the star of the zoo. He has his own cage. What else would he do? He would kill himself if he didn't have this. With all that guilt."

"Barry, are you a psychiatrist?" she asked.

"Why do you ask?"

"You seem to have such insight into human behavior."

"No, I'm a veterinarian."

"Well, there's certainly a lot of dogs barking here tonight. Do you mind if I have you for an appetizer?"

Gene bristled. "Well, what about me?"

"Oh, sloppy seconds are all around, just relax."

Carol took me by the hand, and we went up the spiral staircase to a gorgeous bedroom with a panoramic view. On the huge bed were two other women in the 69 position.

"Do you mind if we use part of the bed?" I asked them.

One of the women looked up. "The water's fine," she said. "Jump in."

A woman named Linda went to the Botany Club. She asked for more alcohol, more drugs. She had a great time and everything was voluntary. There was no rape, there was no forcing. Maybe she had buyer's remorse afterwards. But the rules were ironclad. No one would have touched her against her will.

Drunk, she had sex with four men, and then passed out on a huge pile of fur coats. When she woke up, her dress was up to her chin, her legs were covered with semen, and she was quite disheveled. Because of all the drugs she had taken, she couldn't remember what she'd been doing for the past four hours. So she supposed, not unreasonably, that she had been raped.

She heard noises, crashed out the door to the cloakroom, went outside, and found herself in the middle of a Botany Club orgy. Everybody was in different positions of debauchery. Couples were in ménages, two or three at a time, singles, doubles, and various erotic positions, watching a very high-end softcore erotic movie. There were drugs on the table, including cocaine, and the room smelled of amyl nitrate. Broken bottles were lying around. She had awakened into a nightmare.

With no shoes on, she started running toward the terrace's open sliding door, screaming. "I got raped!" she yelled.

There were flower boxes on the terrace. Linda ran sideways and hit a flower box, almost taking a tumble off the veranda. Two husky guys and I grabbed and restrained her, as she panicked and writhed.

"Come on," one of them told her. "We'll help you get dressed and take you wherever it is you need to go."

They calmed her down and took her home. I have often wondered, over the three decades since that incident, what would have happened if we hadn't caught Linda in time, and she had slipped off the terrace and fallen from the balcony to the concrete below. Too high a price to pay, but would that have brought any one of us to our senses?

•◊•◊•

The Botany Club was in a four-story commercial building in the Flower District, above a wholesale flower shop. Past a long aisle of plants to the back, there was a small, grimy Irish pub. Suddenly, it was like central casting: everyone was beautiful and well-dressed, and that was where we networked and planned our parties.

There were encounters in the doorways, before you entered the club. Many members went into the alley for a quickie, so they didn't start the orgy with a loaded gun. We were like dogs. People opened their windows, screaming, *"What are you doing down there, you animals? Don't you have any shame?"*

A new Mercedes would pull up and back into a no-parking zone. A stunning woman would emerge and go into the flower shop. And the chauffeur would go across the street to the Greek all-night restaurant to get a cup of coffee.

In the Botany Club, people were milling around, dancing, some throwing darts, and some playing pool at a small pool table. Some were eating hamburgers and steaks. Christie, the young lady I had brought, was elegantly dressed like everyone else, and I was in black tie. We were getting some attention.

The Wishing Hour was coming close; it was Friday night at nine-thirty. The Botany was in full blast. Everybody wanted us to sit at their table. Out of the corner of my eye, I saw two beautiful girls dancing together. It started as a threesome with a guy, but they pushed him away, and he fell over on a chair, drunk.

I continued to watch the two young women dancing very close.

I sat by the window watching taxis pull up and people getting out. A bum washed the windows of one taxi.

And more people came.

An orgy was in progress in the ten-room apartment. Beautiful Botany Club people were dancing and eating, and while some watched a basketball game on TV, others were in various rooms on top of each other. Girls in bras and panties were making popcorn and pizza. It was an orgy, but other things were going on. Some people were reclining on furniture, resting up. A tall young man exhausted a female partner. "Next!" he called, and another woman took her place.

It was Friday night at one in the morning. The nineteen-year-old who I brought to the swing was running around, showing her wares to everybody. New meat, new taste, new vitality.

I was so bored! I pulled Christie off two men, and a scuffle broke out.

"I'm leaving," I told her.

There was a general protest among the other men nearby.

"No, I didn't get her yet!"

"Hey, she's new!"

"Sorry," I said, "we're leaving. Next! Next place! We're going to have some dinner. No more show and tell. It's over, time to go."

There were more protests. "Oh, you prick!"

"She has a choice," I said. "Christie, you wanna stay?"

"Noooooo. I wanna be with you."

I took my little nymphette by the hand. "That's it, guys! Nobody's getting any more of this!"

How selfish, but that was that. I was the ringleader. The other contestants were asking to please let her play. *Give me a reason! Why should I let her play? I brought her here. She's mine. I control her. I got her addicted!*

The next weekend, I took Christie to a party on a yacht on the Hudson that was owned by a financier. We all had a fine time, and he invited us to meet him the next week at a restaurant he owned on the West Side. He said he would be there, but his *birddog* Randy would be there, too. You couldn't miss her. She was blonde and six feet tall.

The terminology was flattering: one sent out a birddog to bring back the bird—in other words, Randy was his procurer; it was her job to "procure" the woman accompanying me by luring her away from me over to him. He was gaming me. But since he was fat and bald, it worked the other way around: I took Randy away instead.

There she was, right out of *Elle*: gorgeous, elegant, and a wannabe lesbian. We all got together, went back to my apartment for the weekend, and Randy and I became an item. She wanted me to teach her how to inflict pain, and to tie her up and whip her, and make her crawl. I said, "Why not? I'm unemployed."

She had a fine eye for photography. I saw her portfolio, in which were several magazine covers—not particularly *Voguey*, but avant-garde and offbeat—*The Village Voice*, *Midnight Blue*...

She took me to her doctor, who gave out scripts for disco biscuits (Quaaludes) and amphetamines. For fifty dollars you got one script for each. It was a sleazy office on St. Mark's Place. He said he was a doctor and had all the plaques, but I didn't believe him. He asked me a few silly questions, took my temperature, and I told him that I had a pain in my back and needed something to keep me up. I said thank you, paid and left. I gave Randy the uppers, and she gave me the "biscuits."

Many doctors did this, from Park Avenue to the Bronx. It was an epidemic. People were so stoned in supermarkets they crashed their carts. At my own market at 69th and 3rd, people were putting food in my cart rather than in theirs. They talked in slow motion.

We were warned not to take them with alcohol. Of course, our modern medicines say the same thing, but disco biscuits and two drinks? People were introducing themselves to other people and vomiting on each other. What could be worse than making love to a beautiful woman, and she reaches over for a cigarette and suddenly vomits all over your chest?

I said, "Please don't come into my apartment and take biscuits, if you've been drinking. I can't party, and make love, and wear a raincoat. It doesn't work."

I was divorced at this point, and my apartment was a two-bedroom, two-bath on the East Side with gorgeous rugs everywhere—oversized pillows, lots of plants, one glass table and four chairs, with a seduction cave, and the rest of it was baby-proofed. Except for the dining room chairs, there was no place to sit; you had to lie down or crawl around, once you got through the front door. And it had a great stereo system.

One bedroom was set up for my kids on the weekend, with a TV and pull-out sofas or for "patients" that Dr. Dollowicz, Mr. Cocaine pusher himself, had sent over who couldn't get home.

It was perfect for debauchery. The bedroom had a huge king bed and a box spring right on the floor with vibrators plugged in on either side. It was an operating room. This is where I brought Randy. I knew about some of the equipment from Ginger and had been pleasantly educated, over and over, at the soirées we had with the girls. But it really wasn't my thing to inflict pain on anybody. Randy taught me how to do it to enhance her orgasms and her craziness.

The next weekend, we drove up to Vermont with my kids to my friend Charlie's house. He had a log cabin on a hundred acres that he had hand-built with his son and his friends.

We went out into the woods that afternoon, and she had me tie her to a tree and whip her around her body. She was so white and Aryan-looking that she quickly got blotched. I wasn't into it.

Chapter 12:

Shakin' and Jivin' with the Players

The Camelot was on 45th and 8th. Another building before its time. There, a policeman's horse had bit a doorman in a squabble outside. They rushed the doorman to the hospital, along with his two detached fingers. They had to use a crowbar to pry them out of the horse's mouth.

My job was to manage this building, but it was unmanageable. It was twelve stories high with two hundred units, mostly singles and studios. Many creeps wanted to live there. It was good for a trick pad, for a crash pad, or for foreigners who thought they were on the fashionable East Side.

I met a Cuban couple who wanted to lease a two-bedroom apartment. They told me up front they wanted to have a low-class brothel that would be open twenty-four hours, targeting longshoremen and stevedores. It was twenty dollars for half-and-half. They would give me good money up front, and a percentage. Why not?

It looked like a doctor's office—a lot of chairs in the front. Ashtrays, lamps, newspapers from foreign ports. Girls on one side, boys on the other—the *Choose Your Loser* game. My job was to make sure no other people—police, management—would mess with their business. I would arrive every Friday and pick up my cash and my pound of flesh.

Around the corner on 8th Avenue, near the old Madison Square Garden, was a New York landmark called Small's Paradise. There was also one up in Harlem that I went to on other occasions, but the one on 8th Avenue catered to players and people in the Life: prostitutes, drug dealers, pimps, thieves, and gangsters.

In the front there were businessmen straggling over from the Garden. That would be before eleven o'clock. Most got too drunk to stay around for the action or were too white to fit in. Small's served delicious chicken, ribs, and greens all night long. Or anything else you wanted, all night long. Hot and cold, black or white, well done or medium. Or extra rare, if you were really hungry.

It looked like any other West Side hangout, with booths and a long bar. A blind black man in a derby, suspenders, white shirt, and sunglasses would sing the blues, accompanying himself on a stand-up piano.

I was the only white man there, except for one other fellow sitting at the corner of the bar: Pretzel Man. He was slumped over in a gentle drool, his head buried in a plastic container full of pretzels—feeling no pain, and ignored as if he were a pet. The other customers would pat his head when they came in.

Some pimps wore leather jackets. Others wore pelts from animals that looked like they came from the Bronx Zoo. They were made from zebra, lamb, mink, chinchillas—with matching hats. There were more diamonds and diamond watches in the room than at store windows in the Diamond District, and the odor from all the different colognes was enough to give you a migraine.

And there they would all be, shakin' and jivin' in a room full of smoke to Barry White, who couldn't "get enough of your lovin'."

And everybody had a gun.

My first time there, everyone watched me. Some of the brothers were muttering.

A waitress brought me my order of ribs, chicken, beer, and cornbread. I tried to eat the ribs first, but they were too hot, and I dropped one on the floor, mumbling to myself. The waitress stepped back with her hand on her hip, staring. I picked up a piece of chicken, started to chew, and it was delicious. I chewed, chewed—and it wouldn't go down. I spat it into a napkin.

The exasperated waitress finally blurted out, "Casper, what are you doing here? Get the fuck out of here. You don't know what good food is!"

Now some of the brothers were muttering. Another customer, Cletus, was chatting with his friend, Dog, at the bar. Cletus was a rainbow: a large, imposing black man wearing a three-quarter length black leather coat, a lime green suit, a purple shirt, yellow alligator boots, and a matching black hat with a red band.

"What is that?" I heard Cletus ask. "That some garbage that wandered in here?"

"You sure he's not a cop?" Dog replied. "Looks like undercover to me."

"That boy's so stupid he shouldn't be breathin' our air."

Cletus and Dog came over. Cletus sat down across from me, shades on, toothpick stuck between his teeth, diamonds on every finger. He lifted up his sunglasses, looked at me hard: a white man in a house full of pimps. I was begging to be rolled.

"Who gave you permission to come into our house?" he demanded.

I looked at him and belched. "Excuse me," I said. "What is your name, sir?"

"What the fuck's the difference what my name is?"

"Anyway, since you won't tell me who you are, thank you very much for having me in your house for dinner. I hope I didn't insult you by not being able to eat, but I don't feel particularly well."

Cletus considered me incredulously for a moment, and his face relaxed. He smiled.

"Dog, I think our bro' here needs some fresh air. Let's go out and check traps and pull some line in, take him with us. Go get our hog."

Moments later, the "hog" pulled up in front of Small's: an outrageous Cadillac Seville, with grill, customized with leg plugs—chrome extensions coming out of the sides—purple, pink, and red, sliding roof, and continental kit.

A young woman walked over to us.

"Sweet Potato," Dog said, "get in that fuckin' rig. Get in."

Sweet Potato was five-eight with a great Afro, ebony skin, hoop earrings, a halter top, no underwear—fabulous looking and dumb as a doorknob. She had sunglasses on to hide a black eye.

"Uh-huh," she muttered.

Sweet Potato got in the hog with Cletus, Dog, and me.

I was in the front seat, and Dog was in the back with Sweet Potato, whose Afro nearly touched the roof, as Cletus drove down Lexington Avenue.

Cletus and Dog were wearing pimp hats, and they passed me one.

Barry White was going "deeper and deeper," while the other three bobbed their heads in unison.

There were girls on many corners, and as the hog moved up the street, they ran out like fish joining a school. Obviously they'd been lounging, and when they saw the mac-man coming they knew to get to work on that corner—to get back on the stroll, quick!

Cletus leaned out the window screaming obscenities at the ladies of the night.

"Bitch! Ho! Work! I need money, honey! I need money, honey! Dog, you know I'm six deep?"

Dog smiled. "Oh! Ho! Ho!"

"Bitch!" Cletus said to Sweet Potato. "Hand me the toot."

Sweet Potato took out a little vial with a spoon, removed a big portion of cocaine and put it in Cletus's left nostril, then his right. She passed it back to Dog and did the same for him.

I asked Cletus, "Could she do that to me?"

Sweet Potato made a face. Cletus gave her a look. She complied.

Cletus smiled. "Anything you say, dude!"

Sweet Potato gave me a generous amount of *one and one*—a sniff of cocaine in each nostril. My eyes started tearing.

The music was swaying. I looked at Cletus, Dog, and Sweets, who were bopping and weaving to the music, and started bopping and weaving with them.

•◊•◊•

Around the corner, in the fifties off Central Park West, was another club called Miss Lacy's. This was a posh, overdone New Orleans restaurant. People dressed sharp. That's where you took your top ho, your main woman, and had your champagne and showed off your jewelry, your threads, and your roll. Of course, most of the pimps knew me. I was their banker, their landlord, and their party friend. And they knew they could trust me.

One morning at about four, I stopped by Miss Lacy's to pick up some pocket money. As I walked in, two cops walked out. They asked me if I was lost, but I assured them I knew exactly what I was doing and that my judgment was not impaired in any way from alcohol or any substance—which was the truth, since I had just woken up.

It was a small, quaint, New Orleans-style place, with many gas lamps, built-in banquettes, a little dance floor with a jazz group, and cocktail waitresses in Vegas bunny outfits. A spiral staircase led upstairs to a small, intimate, second story where everyone was doing drugs. They were having a birthday party for my client, Fast Black. He was up on the stage making speeches. They were pouring champagne on him while Barry White was screaming away on the jukebox, and the girls were gyrating in their flimsy costumes, and the men's hats were flapping in the air. There was crushed felt, suede, buckskin—even a Davy Crocket raccoon hat. I often ventured out around four in the morning to pick up rent money, because two hours later I'd go out fishing. I was in my boots, dungarees, and fishing coat, and, I must say, I probably looked a bit out of place in a joint full of pimps.

It was time for breakfast, so I ordered a screwdriver. As I sat in my plush chair and looked around, I had the sensation that I was on another planet or waiting to be lifted off or left behind. I couldn't quite understand, at that moment, what I had in common with all those people, except the greed for money. It was enough.

Calvin and Benny, two very well-dressed players in the night, were arguing about a lady sitting between them named Karen.

"Listen, Benny, you mother fuckin' dumb coon," Calvin said. "I don't care if she chose you. She owes me some money. I just got her a new fur. And she been with me for five years. And it don't look good, her leavin' me."

"Calvin," said Benny, "she just a ho. An' we're just talkin' about money. And she chose! And she chose Benny! And that's the way it is. And I'm here like a man, in your face, givin' you the truth. Now, if you can't take the truth, that's your problem, motherfucker!"

"Nigger, I'll cut the side of your face," Calvin replied. "Talk that shit in this club like that in front of all my friends."

"You cut me, and I'll be throwin' your bitches off terraces."

The third man sitting at the table was Snake—sort of the mediator, the oldest pimp in the room. Gray hair and a gray goatee. Snake looked at Calvin, shaking his head.

"You know the rules, Calvin. She chose, you froze. That's the way it is."

It was getting light out, time to go fishing, so I got up and left.

•◊•◊•

It was a crowded Friday night at Plato's Retreat, and people were lined up on 73rd and Broadway at the old Astoria Hotel, the classic building where writers, artists, and judges lived at the turn of the century. Ginger and I moved toward the front of the line, where I slipped a hundred-dollar bill into the doorman's hand. Inside there were Corinthian columns, art deco statues of Michelangelo's David, WPA murals, and black and white marble floor tiles.

As we headed down the old stairs, people were coming up in various states of dress and undress, in evening gowns, and jumpsuits. It felt like Halloween again.

Downstairs there was a Turkish bath where they used to give massages. People were smoking cigarettes, talking, and eating. People lolled in various pools and lay on *chaises longues*, with sheets wrapped around them, the air smelling of Lysol and perfume. *Saturday Night Fever* disco songs blared out.

Ginger and I found an excellent viewing position.

"Ginger?" I asked, "What do you think?"

She considered my question. "My first impression? They look like a very bored and lonely group."

"Hmm, interesting. They do look bored. Well, I'm getting bored, too. Let's go have some dinner."

"Barry, I thought this was your thing?"

"I thought so, too, but maybe not anymore..."

The doorman at Dr. Dallowicz's building was very busy, as people came home from work and had to be let in, and at the same time, people asked him to get cabs for them. A woman resident came in, checked her mail, and complained to him that "they" kept putting "the wrong fucking mail in her fucking mailbox," and she was tired of telling them—and she threw the mail at him.

Dr. Dallowicz, who insisted he was the cousin of Salvador Dalí and had assisted and trained with him in his late years, lived in a building in the West Fifties on 8th Ave. It was a luxury doorman building, but it was lucky the doorman didn't get shot half the time opening cabs and darting in and out. He was very much in harm's way, as the area was very dangerous for pedestrian traffic after a certain hour. There were junkies, mac-men, and confidence men slinking all over the streets. I was a regular.

It was a small one-bedroom apartment with a raised-platform dining room and odd Dalí-style paintings all around. There was a pot of pasta sauce brewing, the telephone was ringing, and people were slipping in and out of the bedroom for discreet transactions. Others were sitting around doing the free drugs and telling stories they thought were funny.

I smelled the spaghetti sauce. "Ah, the sauce smells great!" I licked the spoon. "Are we going to have dinner or breakfast?"

At the moment, there were five people interacting in the living room: an ex-prizefighter, a model, a cross-dresser, a garment center salesman, and a chef who was wearing a toque instead of a chef's hat.

The phone rang. The bell rang downstairs as they came and went—kisses, hugs, handshakes with money exchanged, hushes in the bedroom, a little triple-beam scale always in use. The goods were out on the table. Dallowicz always had plenty of cut cocaine for the locals who came there just to use and abuse—the pure stuff was in the bedroom. You never knew who you were going to meet there, and at all hours people were coming out of the bedroom in bathrobes. We were friends for years, and I still remember his phone number thirty years later. Unfortunately, one day it wouldn't ring and nobody would know where he was. The doctor is now missing.

It was about three in the afternoon. My eyes were pasted closed, my throat hurt, my whole body shrieked with exhaustion. I didn't quite know where I was. I opened my eyes and on the ceiling was the most hellacious art I've ever seen—it looked like Kandinsky, Picasso, and Salvador Dalí—all hung over. There were lumps all over the floor—they were people. I hoped they weren't dead. Had I killed them? Had I made love to them? God, where was the bathroom? Oh my, somebody was sleeping in the bathtub. I didn't care—pissing on them. What was for breakfast. Pasta.

Darkness. A match sizzled to life. Flame, the front end of a cigarette. A long, deep drag in the darkness.

This is what I see at night, because I don't sleep. A flower shop turns into an orgy room. I don't know what's real or not anymore, and I'm in so much pain.

Another deep drag. And I exhale.

Chapter 13:

Were You in Line at Studio 54?

There was an enormous line outside a club on West 54th Street. A huge security guard stood at the front door, people were screaming, photographers were shooting. There were limousines and lights, as a few people were let in at a time. It was the late '70s.

People shouted to the security guard, "Steven! Steven! Please let me in! Please let me in! You remember me?"

Steven paid no attention—he was spitting, scratching his crotch, and picking his nose. He gestured occasionally, pointed to a few people and admitted them. He okayed either very beautiful singles and couples or people who were dressed outrageously.

I was in line observing all this, and suddenly this guy pointed to me.

"You!" he shouted. "Okay!"

And before I realized what was going on, the line opened for me, and I was hustled into Studio 54.

The building seemed to be gyrating. As I walked through the lobby, I could see it was an old theatre.

I entered the restroom to piss. It didn't say *Men* or *Women*— just *WC*. I was confused because there were men and women in there. They were giggling, and doing lines of cocaine.

I noticed a gorgeous woman named Crystal Meth go up to a urinal. She lifted up her dress and started to urinate. She had a huge appendage and noticed my surprised stare.

"So I haven't been completed yet," she said, glaring at me. "What's *your* problem?"

Moments after I left the restroom, I was mingling with the glitterati in the havoc of Studio 54. The male bartenders were dressed Chippendale-style. There were couches all around the huge dance floor, and up on the ceiling was a huge silver moon with a human face. Sparkles dripped into his nose. The sound system was deafening, the floor was pulsating. Photographers and paparazzi roamed the rooms with cameras.

People were copulating in the seats.

A beautiful blonde walked over to me, grabbed my hand, and asked if I'd like a disco biscuit. She gave me a Quaalude. Ten minutes later, I sat in the middle of the dance floor, spinning around on my ass.

Outside, as usual, a crowd was frantically hustling to get in, as Steven nonchalantly ignored them.

I was there. Studio 54. A hundred nights in a row. It was my office. And we called it "Studio."

In the beginning, they couldn't get an alcohol license, so we all sat there at the bar, drinking club soda and ginger ale. There were no lines outside, just a few press parties.

At first, the bartenders were starving. They had no fives, tens, or twenties to stuff down their little satin pants, to lift up the corner and show the bulge. They were bored.

Then it changed. It caught on.

I'd see the same faces in that line week after week, jumping, screaming, showing cleavage, showing butt. It just didn't work. If you had the look, you were in. If you didn't, goodbye.

The floor was slippery from sweat. Dancers lost drugs from their pockets. There were people around the dance floor who waited for something to fall. And they swooped down like an eagle, grabbed a vial, and ran. Sometimes they crashed heads together. It was hilarious. I enjoyed it so much that I brought extra vials with cut in them and purposely dropped them.

Coke whores came up to me like cats, rubbing against my leg and purring, their eyes bloodshot. "Hi, honey! You got a toot?

You got a taste for Mama? We could have a great night..." If you were stupid or kind enough to give them a vial instead of a one-on-one, they'd come back ten minutes later with almost none left and say it had spilled. I think some of them tapped it out into a hundred-dollar bill and threw some cut in there, so it looked like something happened.

I would just throw them a vial and tell them to knock themselves out. It was 90-95 percent "cut"—highly diluted, usually with baby laxatives. They didn't know the difference.

That went on everywhere. Many offices, many classrooms, most parties. I can still feel the meows and the hot breath.

I liked the ones who came up to me and said, "Hey, big boy, you wanna taste? I got the pure!" And I would say, "Ain't buyin', but I might be tryin'!" Sometimes it was a home run, sometimes I was just being polite. Sometimes, after I had one woman with me, she whispered in my ear, "Could my girlfriend come, too? We work better as a pair. Or my two girlfriends? We work better as a threesome." By the time I got out, I could have four or five hanging on to me. We couldn't all get in the cab.

Thank God, there was always the Botany Club for a drop. They'd always take some women off my hands.

•◊•◊•

In 1981, my favorite stop around the corner was still the house of the infamous Dr. Dollowicz. He wasn't really a doctor, though. Just our doctor. There was no line, and there were no turnaways at the doctor's. He was always ready to dispense.

He'd open the elevator in the middle of the night, bleary-eyed, and there was invariably the smell of pasta, red sauce, and sausage. I could almost see the trail of tomato sauce down the hall.

I never knew what he'd be wearing when he opened the door. He could be stark naked or in a tuxedo with no pants on. I never warned anybody; I wanted them to be surprised. Many people stayed for days, some for weeks. The Doctor called me and thanked me. The Doctor was in.

•◊•◊•

The first time I met Dr. Dollowicz, I was running a showroom on 3rd Avenue, and one of the salesmen I befriended, who later lost his eyesight at a three-day orgy at the Botany Club, knew him from their days in Brooklyn when they had a little soapbox with roller skates on it that went uphill and downhill. He told me that Dr. Dollowicz was on parole and needed somebody to vouch that he worked for him. I didn't want to get involved, but after talking to the doctor, I thought, *How much trouble could I get into?* He was an artist, intent on copying Dalí's work, and I needed somebody to do renderings for my samples. So I put him on the books. It worked out for him; he got off probation, and they left him alone.

Dr. Dollowicz was on the social scene. He was the social secretary for the heir to a massive blue-blood retail chain fortune, who was the world's worst businessman. I believe he lost $300 million on his ventures. But he was addicted, and the doctor supplied him beautiful, young girls for his huge Park Avenue apartment.

Dr. Dollowicz hid girls in different closets, and tried to give them the old in-and-out when Hunt wasn't looking. Hunt wandered around, calling out to him, "Jeffrey! Where are the women? I can't find them! Please get me the women! They're missing!"

I recently went to the Salvador Dalí show at the LA Museum. It made me sad to recall how hard Dr. Dollowicz unsuccessfully tried to copy Dalí's work. He wasn't that talented as an artist, but he was a good showman who was always in trouble with a relationship.

•◇•◇•

I ran into Edie and Andy constantly at Studio 54.

"Do you want to go to a party?" Edie asked me once, from a lounge chair, when I was coming out of the bathroom.

"No," I said, "there's a party in my head."

"Wow, cool," she said. "Sit down, let Andy look at it. Andy!" she called to Warhol. "Come over and see the party in Barry's head! Look in his eyes!"

We were all very stoned, and the music was screaming.

I saw Andy again and again at Christina's place and at many parties—he was all over. And Edie and Christina got along well, since they both babbled nonsense at each other. They seemed to have an understanding.

It was Saturday night. Pamela, a relatively short-lived girlfriend, was in from LA. It was raining hard, but I bragged about how I could get us into Studio in less than a minute. We pulled up, jumped out of the cab. Huge line, of course. Steven was standing on his box. "Hey guy, how're you doing?" Of course he recognized me; he was soliciting from my list. He screamed, "Fire marshals inside, it's packed! We can't let you in right now!"

"Drip drip drip," went the mascara. She was pissed. My satin boots were getting wet, and I was really pissed, too.

Two huge limos pulled up. Bodyguards opened the doors and out came Liz Taylor and Richard Burton. They were escorted in immediately. Steven gave me the look, and we ran as quickly as we could to get in before the Red Sea closed behind us.

Motherfucker, the place was empty. There was just a skeleton crew waiting for people to come in, and a few of Merv the Perv's friends, sliding around the columns with their vials tucked in their panties.

The photographers had all been shooting the whole thing outside. It was a setup to get the stars' photos. Pamela called me an asshole. Poor Pamela. She was signed for the part in *Charlie's Angels* that Cheryl Ladd got. She was cast, and had the part, and then they said, "Sorry! We're gonna give the part to Alan Ladd, Jr.'s wife instead of you. You understand."

I met Pamela when I was still renting high-end furnished apartments. She was a real Charlie's Angel—beautiful, smart, and talented. It was a good time for me, because I didn't have a main squeeze, and we started dating immediately. She moved in, but I knew she had to go back to Hollywood to pursue her career. So we did the back-and-forth thing for a while.

We were always laughing in bed, ordering food, and just having a great time.

She flew back to California, and since I had business there, I told her I would meet her. She lived around the corner from UCLA, in a duplex, and had a Rolls-Royce and an Excalibur, beige and powder blue. She was a fine athlete, and dragged me to the UCLA track every morning. Thank God, I had some blow for the energy. She wasn't a druggie. She knew everybody on the UCLA track team, and helped them with stretching exercises and limbering up.

She tried to get me back in shape. I ran around the track and up and down the stadium chairs. I hated it.

We drove up to Morro Bay in that beautiful Excalibur, and we spent the weekend eating seafood and making love, but I had to go back to New York, and I lost interest in her. She wanted me to meet her relatives, who owned a bank on Balboa Island. She thought I should get involved with them in business. The whole thing terrified me. I was still hooked on the Life.

Then an illness changed everything. It's a four-letter acronym—AIDS, or SIDA in Spanish.

Imagine walking into a club, seeing a beautiful man or woman, and knowing that there was an excellent chance you could have sex with each other. There was excitement in those bars, and possibility. There might have been a little smoke in the air, but there was no fear. Now, ninety days later, you could be on your way to dying.

People had been able to go out and satisfy their dreams. They worked hard, and they could play hard. There were no repercussions. There might be emotional attachments, incidents, and, of course, there could be death, but it would be a bullet or a knife, not a virus creeping into you and killing you.

Open most magazines. They're selling everything with sex: clothes, jewelry, cars, lifestyle… It's all wrapped around a pair of breasts or a hard penis.

I'm not saying disco biscuits, cocaine, and alcohol didn't add to the illness. If you took too many of these stimulants, there'd be no sex anyway. But a taste got you ready, got you hot, took away inhibitions, and made you ready for the hunt.

It wasn't, at first, about the sex. It was more about the curiosity, about what it was like with everything off—makeup, brassieres, underwear, trousers, pants, and suits. Curiosity.

I got jaded, though, with the Botany Club, Plato's Retreat, and parties in the middle 70s—around the Studio 54 times. You didn't have to take people's clothes off. They did it for themselves. They jumped into a party and that was it; everything came off.

There was too much to see, it was too fast, and not sexy. It was the marketplace, and it was all there. There was no guessing. It was a simple nod of the head, and a nod back, and you were in a cab, off to a situation, a mansion, a boat, a party, for days. It became years.

I would go to a supermarket to buy milk and dog food, and I would be gone for two days. I don't know if it was irresponsible, dangerous, diseased, or addictive, but I wasn't alone.

I lived in a building on the 60s, on the East Side, that had four pubs on four corners. I knew four bartenders with four phones who would call me when there were women and drugs they knew I'd like, and send them up—or I'd go down and get them. It was too easy.

Everybody I knew went out, and they weren't afraid. There was no AIDS. Nothing mattered but a good time. And there were great drugs, easy to get. It was the frequency and accessibility of flesh and narcotics—like a club sandwich.

I think that all tabloid magazines and tabloid television are so popular now because people are bored—locked down. They can't go out, they can't let themselves loose, they work 12 hours a day, spend at least two hours in traffic, they're on antidepressants, junk food, junk books, and junk movies.

Studio 54: I got in, I heard the music, and I was safe. And when I walked through the doors, it was a shot of adrenaline—one, because I got in; two, because the sound system was incredible; three, because I could mingle with royalty, celebrity, and degenerates; four, because sexuality oozed from the walls; five, because the money flowed; and six, because it was a separate fraternity. I was in. Once I got through that front door, I was treated like a regular.

It was a special world, and the rules were different. There was no violence, and I never saw anybody get thrown out. I saw people pass out—found sleeping in the balcony under the chairs when they went to clean up at six—and they were left to sleep it off. There were so many famous people that there wasn't much head-turning. And at the private parties, the costuming and the sets were spectacular and outrageous. But later, there was always talk like, "You should have been there! You know who you missed?" It was very hard to outdo the celebrity factor because in a few minutes you were nobody. Somebody had trumped you.

The dress code stretched from half-naked to tuxedos and evening wear. People tried to dress outrageously to get in—so it was "Halloweenist." And it had an overtone of homosexuality; there was always a good mix of gays, which made it more interesting.

It was international—many different languages were spoken at the tables (a lot of French, Italian, and Japanese). And the sound system was driving. And we had the music of the times: disco.

The music was positive because there was nothing to be worried about. There was no AIDS, there was no war, there was plenty of money, it was New York, it was Broadway, and it was unique. The harder it was to get in, the more people wanted to. It was that simple... and grand.

Everybody was happy, or seemed to be. Invariably, they were high, too. And naturally the music reflected what was going on. We were dancing. People didn't just come in and sit on their asses and get drunk. They were out on the floor—in all sizes and shapes.

People arrived in limousines, on foot, on roller skates, and on bikes. I remember arriving and taking my skates off and putting them in my backpack.

The people waiting in line got wet, got cold, screamed, and yelled. They had their own party, because they knew each other. There were pushy out-of-towners who tried to buy their way in: no, no, no. They were making so much money, but you couldn't bribe your way in. If the club owners considered you unattractive, they didn't want you inside, and a one hundred dollar bill meant nothing.

Once you were inside, night became day and there was fantasy, with or without permission. Walking in was like shedding your skin. You could throw away your personality and your inhibitions—unzip them all, leave them in the lobby, and jump into the pool. It didn't matter: you were in. Anything could happen.

There were no problems with the police, and nobody got busted for being underage. I never heard of anybody having a problem there; they knew how to oil the machinery of New York.

Because of Christina's list, I was one of the original fifty people there. I was just Barry, and I had my automatic—there was no frisking at the door, and you could go in with your gun.

Everybody knew about Studio 54. It was someplace people wanted to go—or at least take a peek, if only to see if the newspapers were exaggerating.

Then it came crumbling down. The owners were indicted and went to jail, where they died from AIDS. It was a complete fall from grace.

But I was there at the beginning, and I was willing to drink club soda when nothing was going on. Besides, it was right around the corner from my drug supplier.

Monday and Tuesday, if you weren't known, and if you begged and jumped long enough, there was a chance you'd get in for an hour. But there were people there who got in on Tuesday who didn't get in on Friday or Saturday—those nights were for the A-List. If you got in and you weren't supposed to be there, you left, quickly. You didn't fit. You couldn't deal. It didn't work. People ran around with gold jockstraps and chains all over them. No point in coming if you couldn't handle the scene.

Studio 54 was entertainment, and it changed every night. It was a special world. You got in, you heard the music, and you knew you were safe for the night.

This was my survival formula:

The first thing in the morning, I needed to do a couple of lines of coke. Then I took some protein powder, a banana, a couple of eggs, blended it all up, drank it down, put on my sweats, my sneakers, slid out the door, and took a nice jog up the FDR Drive—three miles up and three miles back. I came home, took a hot shower, got dressed, went to the office across the street, had a cup of coffee, split a Quaalude with my partner (a half, not a whole, just to get the buzz going), and then I did a couple of more lines. In the afternoon, I had a nice Italian lunch—a lot of pasta, some bread, and a couple of glasses of wine. I came back and snorted a couple of lines. When they wore off, I went upstairs, slept until about one in the morning, put on my leathers or my roller skates, and spent the night at Studio 54, at the Mattress, or roller skating around behind cabs, holding on with gloves, going from cab to cab around the city. I came home when it got light, had a Valium, a Rémy Martin or two, and went to sleep.

That's the way I lived, and I'm still here. This formula was only for during the week. Because on the weekend, the kids came. And then it was no drugs until Sunday night: back to Chinese food, pizza, and an occasional trip to the deli. This was the way. I kept to this diet, and life was perfect. I was enlightened and thoughtful and considerate—or so I believed—and so high, I was smiling all the time.

It was my last night at Studio 54, and I sat in the balcony, my feet up over the chairs in front of me.

There were two young women sitting beside me. To my left was an English rocker, and to my right was a man completely covered with tattoos, including his neck and the back of his bald head, wearing all kinds of silver and skull-and-bones rings. They were passing a joint around and a vial of something as well. Everybody was taking a hit. There was a crackle of glass and a pungent odor of ammonia. The two young women seemed to be in the throes of mutual masturbation, and one of them passed her finger under the other's nose. Then they passed the popper around to me and my friends.

We all got flushed in the face and began to curse.

A young man clad only in silk boxer shorts and sneakers came walking down the aisle behind us. He tripped, stumbled, and rolled down the rest of the aisle, laughing.

"What was that?" I asked one of the young women.

"It's whatever you want it to be," she said.

The Tattooed Man leaned over. "It's your connection to the Higher One."

"How old are you?" I asked the young woman.

"What's up?" she replied irritably. "How old are you?"

"I'm just curious," I said. "How often do you come here? And who did you come with?"

"I don't know who I came with," she said, "and it doesn't matter. And I'm always here. 'Cause this is where it's safe. Believe it or not, these people are real."

"Gimme a break, will you?" I said. "What are you talking about?"

"We all want the same thing," she said, "just to have a good time, and no bullshit. We don't pretend we're not what we are. People come and go out of this joint. A lot of these people have jobs, and they can only come out on the weekends. And that's what we live for. Disco is truth! Life is bullshit."

"I think you've got your priorities a little confused," I said.

This annoyed her. "What the fuck is a priority? Do you get high on it? Is that a word or a drug?"

"Now, now, don't get hostile. I'm just trying to find out what's going on."

"Why? Why do you care? You look like you're on the way out."

I sighed. "You couldn't be more right."

It was four-thirty, and the club was closing. The lights went on and off a few times, and we all rose and started walking down to the dance floor. Some of the people around us were sleeping.

Last Dance came on.

"Would you like the last dance?" I asked her.

She brightened. "I'd love it."

"Studio" was one of the great places to scope. You could sit down and watch the scenery, which was never boring, and just laugh your ass off. And you could wander off and come back two hours later, and it would be entirely different. I don't think there was ever a place in New York where there were so many celebrities and exhibitionists under the same roof. It was cultlike. They've tried to duplicate it, but nobody has ever come close. It was a fond farewell to a period of history. Even with all the sex, drugs, and debauchery, there was an optimism and an offbeat kind of innocence that I don't believe we will ever have again.

Chapter 14:

Dancing with Muktananda

I was long divorced from Francesca when I reconnected with my old travel buddy, Weenie.

As soon as I was out of jail, I'd gone to the American embassy in Madrid where they said they were doing their best to get him out, but they were hazy about the details. Then, three months later, Weenie was released. He apparently had a heavy-duty family connection who assisted somehow, but to this day we have never discussed the incident. It was too traumatic. It was like it never happened. We were different people, and that world closed up behind us and suffocated.

When I saw him in California, he had a business going, a large property, and was very involved in the New Age spiritual community. He seemed to have rejuvenated. He said he wanted me to meet somebody named Muktananda, and I said, "The next time you come through New York, call me and we'll talk about it."

Weenie could see that I was troubled and lost, and he figured I could benefit from some spiritual advice. So he told me about Swami Muktananda, who believed that people can control their own destiny and heal themselves.

Muktananda had his ashram in Fallsburg, New York, and would travel around the country, staying in the homes of devotees. Muktananda said you don't need a middleman to get consciousness—you don't have to go to a church, or a synagogue, or to anybody. You just have to be quiet, and ask.

He said with God, the message is always simple—and it comes direct.

When I asked him about Western religion and all the rabbis and priests, who say, "You can't do this, that, anything... and we will show you how to reach God," he said, "I don't want to criticize any Western religion, or any religion, but that's not necessary. There's absolutely no need for a middleman."

I asked him about the Eastern view of women—why they were relegated to such a low position. And he said, "That's not true. We all come from the woman, the mother. And the mother is omnipotent. People have been taught incorrectly. The women in India are very respected. In fact, for a daughter to get married, a dowry is very important in the Eastern religions. It shows the wealth of taking a wife."

He explained that you can receive *shaktipat* (kundalini energy awakening) through the eyes, through touching, or through dreams. He received his through the eyes of his guru.

Now, as I look back at it all, studying comparative religion and reviewing my life today, he couldn't have been more right.

•◊•◊•

My first encounter with Muktananda was on 14th Street. He was giving *darshan* and telling stories, and Weenie, who was now in New York visiting family, arranged an audience for me to be blessed. He got me in line ahead of everybody else, to see Baba. Ginger from the Pleasure Chest was with me. Her breasts were pouring out of her top, which I thought was inappropriate. But Weenie was leering.

Muktananda had a watchman's hat with all the rainbow peace movement colors, pulled down with a red dot (*bindi*) on his third-eye chakra. He looked at me very closely, gave me the peacock feather, passed it to Ginger, asked Weenie some questions, and Weenie said I was an old friend. Then he blessed me.

I didn't think much about it, but, in retrospect, I definitely did feel something from his eyes—a magnetism, a transmission of energy. I can't really say if it was positive or negative, but it was very intense. Did it change me, make me think differently about anything? No. I was a concrete block; stubborn, unfeeling, demented, and on the prowl. The freak was very much alive and well in me.

It was extremely difficult for me to make a decision then. I would get dressed to go out, go down in the elevator, and come back and get undressed—and stay home and want to read a book, which was not my usual fare. Two hours later, I would go out again and be gone for two days. I had no parameters, nothing to rein me in. I had friends who were up all night and all day, and night and day were the same to me as well.

The following summer, Weenie told me that Muktananda was having a retreat in Fallsburg at his summer place, and that it would really be good for me to go there for a weekend to see if I could connect with his way of life. He said he could get me a discount ticket; everybody was paying $250, but I could do it for $125. Weenie always had a deal.

At this point, I was living part-time with a divorced woman with two kids in a fancy condo on the East Side, and just floating. I took a bus up to Fallsburg, which I was not in the habit of doing, as buses were not my thing. It took a lot of willpower, but I didn't bring any drugs with me because I wanted to go cold turkey.

As soon as I got off the bus, I hated it. All the people were wearing polyester or white robes with beads and gold IDs—it looked like bullshit. There certainly were a lot of women there, and they had a lot of hair on their legs. You could have made a living shaving legs there. But a few beauties did catch my eye. There was a book store where they sold his beads, his books, his incense, and probably his suppositories—for people who were really blocked up.

I was there, so I was going to make the best of it. That night they put us in a dormitory on cots, so I didn't sleep well. They woke us up very early in the morning for breakfast, if you could call it that. It was some Indian food, bread and dahl, wet cereal, and instant mango juice.

Finally, they let us in the auditorium and divided us up— women on one side and men on the other—and there he was,

Muktananda, with his little beanie and a gorgeous woman with violet eyes by his side, who was his translator. At least *she* perked my interest.

They did a Q and A for a couple of hours, which was actually pretty interesting. Then they brought out some musical instruments, played a few songs, and then had a break for lunch, another exciting meal. Even the ants didn't want to eat the food. Then they told us we were going to have an afternoon of prayer, meditation, and a blessing. We came back, they lowered the lights, and I remember Baba's disciples locking the doors all around, which I didn't like.

It was dark, as everybody started chanting mantras. They were bobbing, weaving, jumping, thrashing, and speaking in tongues all around me. Nothing to lean against. I really wanted to be on Fire Island—snorting and being with beautiful women.

Muktananda got down from the platform and started with all the girls first, walking up and down tapping them with peacock feathers on their heads, as if he were dusting them off.

I had been told that he was an *Enlightened One*, a healer, even a mind reader—that he was like Jesus. It was a hot afternoon, I was tired, I wanted to go home, and I thought this was the silliest, most ripped-off thing I ever saw. They were all going like sheep to the slaughter.

He walked up the aisle, and everybody was swaying and sweating—some people were spinning in place. Very, very strange.

He walked up to me, tapped me with the peacock feather. *Big fucking deal, thank you for nothing,* I thought.

Then he looked at me, took his hand, and started rubbing my head—clockwise and counterclockwise as if he wanted to screw it off. I didn't know what the hell he was doing, or why.

My hair got all messed up. I straightened it, and tried to find a way to be comfortable. Suddenly, I jumped up, my eyes wide open as if somebody had dropped a burning cigarette down the back of my shirt. A shock went from the top of my neck down to my coccyx. It burned. It hurt. It moved out to my shoulders, to my arms, and to the top of my head.

The last thing I remember was repeating, "Obbidy obbidy obbidy obbidy obbidy…!"

An hour and a half later, I woke up in a pool of sweat. My clothes were soaked; I thought somebody had thrown me in the pool or doused me with water, and a lot of other people were in the same condition. They put the lights on slowly. I really had trouble getting up. My legs were rubbery.

•◊•◊•

I worked my way slowly over to the reception area, where I bumped into Weenie and a bunch of guys and told them what happened. They told me I was one of the chosen ones, and that I should feel honored that he transferred *shaktipat* to me through his energy up my spine, allowing me to have a karmic change. All I'd wanted was a cheeseburger and a Coke. I listened, and for no apparent reason, I walked into the souvenir shop and bought a few candles, some incense, and a picture of him—and his book.

Weenie bragged to everybody how I got the honor, and how it all happened because I was a friend of his. I went out, walked around, and it was time to take the bus back to New York. As I got on the bus, I bumped into a friend of mine and Weenie's, Mike Morton, another lunatic I knew from the streets. He asked me if I wanted some coke for the ride home. I looked at him and said, "I don't do coke anymore."

For the next three months, I lit my little candle every night, put Muktananda's picture in front of me, and did my mantra. My life started to change. The dance had begun. Muktananda had set me free.

I believe that for all his faults, Weenie did put me in a position where I could have my karma changed. He got me to Muktananda, and later to Ammachi, who hugged me. For that I'll always be indebted to him. And he was always ahead of his time when it came to diet and nutrition. Some of my current personal practices come from things he told me about not poisoning one's body. I thank him for that information, and for his personal encouragement to eat healthy.

•◊•◊•

In those moments of enlightenment, I wanted to face what it would be like going to the other side. I didn't have a real understanding of what happens when you pass. Should you be scared? Is it natural? Where do you go? Who's there? Do they have TV? Well, that would be a stretch.

Death is pleasurable, a dreamlike state in which we slip to the other side where there are people waiting for us in unthought-of dimensions. They can perceive, feel, and control things from a distance with their consciousness and energy. They can't really interfere here because everybody has free will, but our loved ones on the other side can find us if they're sensitive, and we can feel them, if we open up to what the signs are. I know this, because I've seen it. And I don't pretend to be psychic or gifted, but I know it to be true. I see my family, my grandparents, my dogs. I see the other dimension. And I try to listen to my intuition very carefully—when I don't, trouble comes.

Weenie used the powers he received from Muktananda for his own selfish interests—to hunt, to gather meat and tender flesh from the young girls he preyed on. He would lie, cheat, and proselytize for another conquest, night and day. Yes, sometimes the gift of power is misused. But there are inevitable consequences to this.

Weenie had a big house in Topanga, fourteen acres with a hot tub and many bedrooms. He had a health food restaurant and a line of health care products. He organized weekends for Muktananda and his guests, and they would stay there. He kept the unwashed bedsheets in a box. He believed that Muktananda's energy had been transferred to the sheets when the guru slept in them, and he kept them to rejuvenate himself whenever he felt he needed a spiritual lift. He'd roll around in the sheets when he felt down, and whether the benefits were merely psychosomatic or not, the process seemed to work for him. He named his first son "Muktananda."

When Muktananda passed in 1982, he gave the Power to the woman with the violet eyes who was his interpreter and her brother, making them the next in line of gurus in that ascension. And then the feuding began. It appears she won. When Weenie went to her *darshan* to see her and experience her intensive help, they asked him to leave. They'd had enough of his games and his tricks. He quickly embraced Amaji, the hugging guru, an up-and-coming new holy woman. I did get to be hugged by her at his house in a private party, and she was wonderful, pure of spirit, and loving. She also hugged my wife and gave her *shaktipat*.

I think before I die, I want to go to Goa, in India. I've been trying to go there for 25 years. Unfortunately, everybody I planned to go with seems to be dying off, like Roger, my acupuncturist. Every year we talked about how we'd have Christmas in Goa, on the beach. I hear that Goa is one of the most magnificent places in the world. The sages and avatars live there, and it is dotted with Christian monasteries. It's a place where the silk road ends, and the hippies would wind up there in winter because it was very cheap and very beautiful, and it had nude beaches and all the drugs you could use.

I also knew of Guru Sai Baba. In one of my ventures, my partner was an older man, Harry Patterson, and he was a devotee. Once in a while they would have their intensives, or meetings, up in the showroom. Harry was a conservative businessman with a little moustache who looked like Groucho. He was the last person in the world you'd think would be going to India to wear pajamas and chant.

He gave me the books about Sai Baba, and I read them. They were about his telepathy and how he could materialize things out of the air—*vibhuti*, jewelry, presents—he transcended reality.

One of my acquaintances, Errol Wetson, the head of the Wetson hamburger chain, was dating an interesting woman. She was an ex-champion skier, an Olympic hopeful, and very beautiful. She had had a terrible accident. An elevator fell, and her spine was compressed. The surgeons implanted a Harrington rod to support her spine because it was twisted, but it caused her constant pain. She was a real trooper. I liked her a lot. Her name was Susan Mitchell.

We went out socially, and I was aware that her physical condition was deteriorating.

I mentioned it to Harry Patterson, and he said, "Why don't we send her to see Sai Baba in India, and he'll help her?"

"Harry, this is a twisted spine. What could the man do?" I asked.

"She believes in miracles," he said.

We told her about him, and then I didn't hear back from her. A few weeks later I bumped into Errol.

"How's Susan?" I asked.

"She's on her way to India."

"Who'd she go with?"

"Herself," Errol said.

It seems when she got to his ashram, it was too crowded to get in, and she was too weak to try, anyway. So she stayed in her room and cried in pain. That night, Sai Baba came to her in a dream and put his hands up and down her spine. The next day, when she awoke, her pain was gone.

Back in New York, she went to Mount Sinai Hospital, where her doctors said something strange had happened: her spine had regenerated and straightened.

In my travels, not a month goes by that I don't meet someone who knew Muktananda, or wish they had. They go to India, to his ashram, to be healed, to be cleansed, and to rest. Or they stop me in midsentence, and say, "You really knew him? He touched you? What did his eyes look like? What color was his aura?" Sometimes, in despair, I am quiet and say his mantra. And when I close my eyes, I see his face.

I can imagine how people who knew Jesus and were touched by him felt about him. People would go to them and ask, "What was he like? Aren't you blessed just to have known him?" At the time, I'm afraid I may have taken Muktananda for granted, but now I feel blessed to have been touched by him, and for him to have changed my life.

Chapter 15:

Kabul, Kabul

I'd known Ivan since we were kids, and I met him again in 1976. He needed to go to Afghanistan because women were buying lamb coats that were very hot in fashion magazines, and he had a connection to buy them. He thought he could make some good money. I had to look at the map to locate Afghanistan. I knew it was next to Iran, but that was about it. I said, "Are you kidding me? They eat Jews for breakfast over there. But go ahead." I got Maddie Paddy, one of my licensed real estate salesgirls, to lend him some money, and off he went to Afghanistan. He made a few bucks on the coats, and while he was there he bought some cheap rugs and sold them at a large profit.

The next thing I knew, Ivan was living in a big apartment, married, and making a shitload of money bringing in rugs, textiles, and antique ethnic clothing, and they were calling him the new Marco Polo. He got a lot of press; Diana Vreeland, the editor of *Vogue*, said he was a genius, and I was happy for him. Ivan had long hair and wore a bear coat over white pajamas. He married a German woman named Brigitte, and they made a lot of money, and he furnished his apartment like a museum—he had elegant taste.

Ivan began to go through his own divorce. I brought women to him at his apartment, and a lot of nice presents. I noticed that he had checks galore from celebrities. Things couldn't have been better for him.

He kept making trips back and forth to Afghanistan, buying fantastic things, and selling to Bloomingdale's. Once, he over-bought and ran out of money. He said if I gave him some money, we could get into the rug business together, since I was getting shot at too much. The Botany was closing then and "Studio" was on the way out.

He brought back some expensive rugs, and we sold them to Bloomingdale's. Then we made a deal with a big rug supplier in the design building on 59th and 3rd across from Bloomingdale's. He gave me a rug book and a huge showroom with a bunch of rugs. Next, we all put some money together, and back he went to Afghanistan.

I didn't know quite what to do, but I learned quickly and I had a great sense for matching things—which surprised me. I got along great with the gay interior designers, the Jewish housewives, and the jet set. My sketchy background, with its parade of misfits to elitists, served me well. Money poured in, and life was good. It was time to build a factory, and Ivan needed my help.

It was time to go to Kabul.

•◇•◇•

I was at JFK International Airport on my first trip to Kabul in 1974. While waiting in the boarding lounge, I met Sandy, a very voluptuous woman with spectacles. She'd gone to Radcliffe. She asked me where I was going, and I told her I was flying to Frankfurt and then on to Kabul.

"I'm going to Kabul, too," she told me. "My dad's a professor at the university there."

"Well, maybe we should sit together," I suggested. "It's going to be a long trip. Do you have all the right equipment?"

"Ahhh," she replied. "I do."

We spent the next eight or nine hours sitting next to each other, probing all the right spots. She knew exactly what to do to the right areas underneath the blanket. She was wonderful.

We got to Frankfurt, exhausted. There was a ten-hour layover, and we checked into the airport hotel. We did the old in-

and-out for a couple of hours, then boarded the plane for Kabul.

Ivan and his wife, Samantha, picked up me and Sandy, in our RV hippie van which I'd sent money over to purchase. I didn't see downtown Kabul—we immediately went up north through the perilous Salang Pass.

It was around my birthday, sometime in February, and it was still extraordinarily cold. I had jet lag and culture shock, but I was ready. I had my long underwear, my bib overalls, my hat, my quilted jacket, and my anti-rabies shot that Dr. Schwartz convinced me to take in case I got bitten by one of the 180-pound mastiffs roaming around.

Ivan dumped us at an old, abandoned motel. It had about eight rooms—square boxes, high ceilings, a stove, and a tea kettle. I had all my clothes on, with three blankets, and it was still so cold that the teapot froze. Good thing I had Sandy to keep me warm.

I hadn't taken any drugs, but I felt strange. I finally fell asleep, and the room started to spin. There was a candle glowing, and I looked up at the ceiling, and there was no more ceiling.

And then they came: the faces, with beards, with white hair, with no hair, with no arms or legs, but long smoke trails. They kept circling around the ceiling, and all around the room, talking to me, and mumbling. They were diving under the bed, over the bed, and around the bed.

I woke Sandy, but she saw nothing. I went back to sleep, but they were still there, these hallucinations. I thought that I'd eaten some bad lamb, or a bad kebab, but physically, I felt fine.

My body lifted off the bed, and I was chasing around the room with them. In my brain I heard a message: *It's not your time yet. You can play, but you must wait.* That was very encouraging.

It seemed to go on for hours. Finally, I fell asleep.

When I awoke, Ivan was banging on my door, telling me it was time to go. Sandy got up and said she hadn't slept that well in years.

I didn't want to mention my experience to Ivan—it was my trip.

We went to the *chaihana*, the teahouse, and had some nice hot sweet tea and some *nan*, their natural round bread, with a whole garlic stuffed in it. They told me that you had to take the garlic every day with the bread, to get rid of all the parasites that you were surely going to get. I went with it, even though it stank—but we all stank.

Next, we walked over to the famous blue mosque in Masar-i Sharif. The beautiful blue and white tiles are supposed to be unparalleled, except in Isfahan, in the great mosque in Iran.

It was magnificent. In the air and around the mosque were thousands of white doves. I kept looking at their faces, and they were so strange, like a 3-D film—they looked as if they were melting. If you squinted, they almost looked like people's faces.

Later, some old wise men told me, through translators, that these were reincarnated souls who had watched over the mosque for thousands of years, as well as people who were killed by Genghis Khan's invading army, and children of Alexander the Great and his band, who left their seed all over the Hindu Kush.

I found I had trouble walking. The air was so heavy, it felt as if it was pushing people out of the way. I'd never felt anything like that before.

We drove over to Balkh, one of the oldest cities in the world, and the birthplace of Rumi, the great 13th-century poet and mystic. A few hundred yards from the old wall was our factory, which we'd built to make rugs.

It was a primitive scene. The walls were all mud and straw, like Santa Fe American Indian mud houses with huge rooms and looms. Seated around them were bizarre-looking warriors; they called them *waraks*, the weavers from that area. They were all drinking tea with opium. Some of them had kohl around their eyes. They wore an assortment of used army clothes and ragged local gear.

We had a little room off to the left, where children spun wool and cotton. A teacher was there, teaching them their lessons. It was hard to believe that the rugs from this little place were being shipped to New York to be sold to the Du Ponts, Angelo Donghia, and Alfred Traub, the president of Bloomingdale's. We also took custom orders.

After lunch, I walked the plank to move my bowels. There were two pieces of wood over a large hole. If you missed, you were in it. The cold wind blew on my ass, blowing down from the Russian Steppes.

Ivan and Sandy and I walked down the street. He showed us the walls and the field where Genghis Khan and Kublai Khan camped in the summer, and where their armies rested.

There was an old man with his ear against the wall. He looked like Methuselah's brother, he was so old and frail. His eyes twinkled. I looked at him, and he beckoned for me to come listen to the wall.

I put my ear to the wall, just like he did. I heard thundering hooves. I'm sure it was some weird illusion, but it did sound like pounding hooves. I repeated it two or three times, but it was still there. I asked Ivan to listen, but he said he didn't do walls.

On the road back to the factory, I kept losing my balance, as if I were walking on the subway, and people were bumping into me.

We picked up several bales of rugs, put them on top of the Volkswagen and headed back down towards Kabul. It was time for me to buy some local gear for my camouflage.

We went to one of the local tailors, where they took my measurements and said they'd have my shirts and pants in three hours. Then we went over to the cobbler, who took my shoe size, and said in the morning they would have boots for me, one needlepoint pair, and two local brown pairs, knee-high.

That night, we went to one of the small hotels and listened to some music. I passed out. I was finished.

•◊•◊•

The next morning, we picked up our gear, gassed up, and headed for Jalalabad, the famous Khyber Pass, the northwest frontier Worestan, where Bin Laden supposedly hid, and then through Landi Kotal, a no-man's-land in the northwest province. The scenery was magnificent, and the mountains were so high and so sheer that it hurt your neck to look straight up.

The road was hellacious. There were about three inches along the edge, and when I peered over, occasionally I saw a burnt-out truck. We couldn't pass anybody—it was supposed to be two lanes, but was really one and a half.

After a couple of hours we stopped at a little kebab stand. We had some kebabs, a couple of glasses of goat milk, some... I don't know what they call them, but they were delicious, made out of dough with some green stuff inside.

Then it was time to light up the pipe. It was the hour of opium. The pipe came out, and we all got wasted. Black opium from Afghanistan will paralyze you. I was pinned to the seat, drooling.

I was fascinated, going past the old Khyber fort. The road was just as Kipling evoked it in *The Man Who Would Be King*: winding and winding, and winding. Finally we arrived in Jalalabad, the breadbasket of Afghanistan. It's like the San Joaquin Valley in California—everything grows everywhere. There were lush, oversized melons, every kind of nut, oranges, raisin groves. Afghanistan was the world's raisin capital.

We pulled over for lunch. We had a salad with all sorts of fruits and vegetables. I was so hungry and stoned, I bit my fingers.

Hours later, we reached the frontier of Pakistan, Landi Kotal. You've probably seen it on television hundreds of times—that's where they make the weapons, and all the shooting takes place. It's like the Wild West. We had to bribe four different people to get through the various checkpoints. Plus, you weren't allowed to bring any Pakistani rupees into the country from Afghanistan, but we had a lot of rugs on the top of our van that we were taking across the border.

Behind us were freaks from all over the world: hippies in Jeeps, school buses, land rovers, Mercedes trucks, people hanging out half-naked, music going on, trucks painted like tie-dye, people hitchhiking with guitars, girls with T-shirts with no bras and short-shorts. Images right out of Kesey's *On the Bus*. Nobody bothered anybody, and everybody had a pass.

The Afghani people couldn't have been nicer, and I was consistently impressed by their integrity. You shook hands and you *really* had a deal. And they were enormously hospitable, always trying to bring you home for dinner. The outlaws looked tough, but they were way too high as they made their guns. They warned me not to cross at night—some people didn't make it. But during the day, it was fine.

As we came down from the mountains, it started to get really hot. We had about a hundred miles to go to Peshawar, another frontier town.

I had wondered why we had three tires on the top of the van. I quickly found out. During the first thirty miles we blew one tire, and we blew another one an hour later. The roads were pitted with rocks, axle wheels, broken gun barrels, and glass jars.

On the same road were people herding sheep and yaks. They scraped our van with their horns and rocked it, as they snorted slime.

We arrived in Pesháwar. We got our rooms and hired bodyguards to sleep outside our doors that night. This was in the '70s, before the Taliban, but we were being careful. We were Americans, and we did have money on us, plenty of money.

The next night, we were back on the road to Lahore. First we stopped in Islamabad, and then in Ráwalpindi. They were gorgeous cities with mansions, and very British, left over from the occupation.

Coming to the main square in Lahore, where the great mosque is, it felt as if ten roads converged. A few stoplights—half of them were out—rickshaws bouncing against the side of the van, people jumping on the roof, showing their missing limbs and eyes. At the lights, when we did stop, they rocked the van.

We tried to ignore it, as we were told. You just pretended it wasn't really happening.

We checked into a beautiful hotel with marble baths and sunken living rooms, and we got cleaned up.

We met Rasheed, who was our guide and our exporting partner. We went over to the Pak Punjan Rug Factory, which had been there for centuries, to have our rugs cleaned and colored, to turn red into gold.

An old man named Joseph invited us for lunch. We all sat on little cots and ate fruits, vegetables, and sweetmeats.

•◊•◊•

The next day, we left for Multán. It was one of the oldest cities in the great Indian empire, before it was divided into Pakistan. We went to a fabulous museum, where they made wonderful wedding tents. Supposedly, Multán is where Alexander the Great got shot in the heel with an arrow.

It was getting hotter and hotter as we headed south towards Karachi. We stopped off at Baháwalpur to pick up some rugs from a local school. We wandered through the bazaar to meet our connection. It was so much stranger than the bazaars I remember in North Africa, where the sky was much brighter and clearer. Here, there were monkeys jumping from rooftop to rooftop, and laundry was hung about everywhere, literally blocking out the sun; in most places, you couldn't see the sky. The streets were much tighter, so you could have trouble even walking two abreast. Many more of the people had mutilations, and malaria was close by—everything was built on swamps. It was darker, deeper, and dirtier.

We were the only white people. They treated us very nicely, but many dark eyes were looking out of the windows at us.

Parrots were flying overhead, goats were shitting on my shoes, and there were flies on top of flies. Thank God we had opium.

I was so very, very high. Everybody was smoking.

The bazaar was so crowded, I couldn't tell if it was day or night. It was all covered over with mats and fabrics, and oh, look, a monkey just came by my head.

We pulled out of there and headed for a chuck, a small village where they made blue and white durrie mats and prayer rugs.

We entered the village as it was getting dark. They put us in various rooms, and we were separated. In the middle of the night, I heard coughing, and screaming, and crying. Thank God I had some valium. I momentarily thought of Sandy, alone in her room.

In the morning, I walked out into the hall, and there were two bodies covered with sheets. No one I knew, but this was not a good sign. Breakfast at the morgue.

After a lot of translating from English to Hindi back to Farsi to English, it appeared we'd landed in the middle of a malaria epidemic. And there was no quinine in the house.

We grabbed our chuck rugs, got in our van, lit our pipes and off we went, hoping we weren't infected.

Obviously, I didn't die.

•◊•◊•

When we first decided to head north, it was my turn to drive.

Of course, it was a British colony, and you have to drive on the left side of the road. I heard many thumps, and I didn't know if I hit a yak, a person, or a goat, but I didn't stop. I just kept going.

About two hours out of Lahore, they made all the cars pull over and told us there was going to be a delay. They believed that Pakistan was at war with India, and they were going to move the troops up. For the next three hours, we saw nothing but military convoys passing us: tanks, rocket launchers, and troops in combat gear. I had gotten myself in the middle of a war!

When the sun came up, they gave an all-clear sign, and we were able to move out. Back to Lahore, back to Peshawar, back through the Khyber Pass, and back to Kabul. The whole trip took about three weeks. Once there, Sandy and I parted ways.

After a few days, it was time to go back to New York. I'd had enough, and my stomach let me know it was unhappy. I took some great pictures, got on the plane, slept in Frankfurt, and flew back to America.

I brought a stomach infection back with me. It started the day I got home, and I had to go to the center for infectious diseases on Fifth Avenue. They took blood and found something they weren't used to seeing, so they put me on heavy antibiotics.

My consciousness was shifting because I felt I had viscerally experienced another dimension in Masar-i Sharif, seeing the old souls in my room and hearing them in the wall. Treading on 5,000-year old streets where Genghis Khan and Alexander the Great had strutted made an impression on me. I realized how young America is, and how old the world is. I also realized that there were other hippies than the ones in Greenwich Village and Woodstock. I had gone to the cradle of civilization to do business, but there I had found seekers who were traveling around the world, looking for God. Everyone I met seemed to be on a spiritual quest. But I went back to my safe apartment in Manhattan, and the drugs, with my own gnawing dissatisfaction, while these people kept looking for God.

All the magazines were talking about Santa Fe as the place to go, the New Frontier. Ivan wanted to go there because there were mountains, and he couldn't go back to Kabul yet.

I went out there and leaned on him to buy his house in Sunlet Hills for very little. Then I came back to New York and started to spiral again, badly. Wearing the white Afghan robes of a hippie businessman, I felt it was time for me to leave. I'd outgrown New York, and it had outgrown me. It's hard to carry a pistol in your pajamas. The chaos, the people, the cabs, and restaurants were all overwhelming. It was a new city compared to the B.C. cities that I'd visited. It hurt me to be in New York. I was ready to leave.

•◇•◇•

On my second trip to Afghanistan, I returned with Ivan, leaving his wife Samantha behind to run the factory. Coming into America on Lufthansa, we both were wearing our white pajamas and needlepoint vests, and Ivan had very long hair and earrings and sort of a tunic dress. He was carrying a bunch of saddlebags.

"Ivan, I hope you didn't bring any shit in there!" By this I meant accidental opium crumbs or leftovers. I had disturbing visions of being arrested at JFK "by accident." Who would believe me?

Ivan and I were back together because I'd sold $77,000 worth of rugs to a Texas client. Our third partner was a Harvard grad who would not pay us our full share for some rugs he sold. He told me that Bloomingdale's only worked on 7 percent, and we should be happy we were making such a huge percentage as it was.

"What the fuck does that have to do with you owing us fifty grand, Frank?"

"I don't have the money to pay you guys right now, you'll just have to wait up the road," he said.

"I just got back off the road," I said. "You don't know how hard it is to get these rugs, and what I have to go through."

Ivan and I made a plan. We would wait for the showroom to close at the design center. The building itself was open on Saturdays, and I knew all the codes.

We had a lot of crappy merchandise stored in a warehouse that was damaged or not primo, and I didn't want it on the floor. We rented a truck, took along our CPA accountant as a front man, got a bunch of laundry bins, and put the old rugs in there. The old switcheroo.

It took us about three hours to bring all the damaged rugs into the showroom and bring the good ones back to our warehouse.

We ended up with two thirds of the good merchandise, which we were entitled to. Plus, we took a half dozen sold rugs belonging to movie stars and Mrs. Marcos, the dictator's daughter, and Bernie would really get fucked if he didn't give them back.

•◊•◊•

Monday morning, when the showroom opened, it looked normal to the unpracticed eye, but once the salesmen tried to show these rugs that had holes and stains in them, and were otherwise unsuitable, I heard Bernie started to scream and jump up and down like a maniac, shouting, "I've been robbed! I've been robbed! Who robbed me?" I didn't show up for work. We contacted our lawyer and the negotiations started.

A few weeks up the road, after some heated negotiations, and after the Embassy from the Philippines and various others complained that they wanted their merchandise, Bernie paid us.

We moved into Morgan Manhattan Warehouse on 81st and 3rd. We had a huge room and hundreds of rugs, and we operated out of there for a couple of months, selling to interior designers that I knew. My life was in the process of changing.

Through a relationship with Albert Hadley, a great decorator and a charming, sincere man, we were able to get a deal with Patterson, Flynn, and Martin at 57th and 3rd. There I met some of the great designers of the world: Mark Hampton, who decorated the White House, Bobby Metzger, the McMillan firm, and Dorothy Draper. Albert was also partners with Sister Parish, the matriarch of the interior design business. He was a very powerful influence on me in his taste and creativity. And I really learned the craft of mixing and matching.

Chapter 16:
Saved by the Bell

It was two days before Halloween, 1981, when my phone rang. It was Joel Leff, the most successful hedge fund manager in New York City at that time. His company was called Atalanta, and I'd met him through my old high school friend, Mark Newman, who was also his partner. Joel was also partnered with Tony Forstmann, who had married Charlotte Ford, so they had that Ford money to invest. Joel went to Harvard, had polio, and looked like a thinner Donald Sutherland. He was a real player, and we'd become good buddies.

"Hey, Bar, there's a great party on the West Side; wonderful ladies, great food—my old friend, Delilah Henry, who was my designer, is the hostess."

"Joe, I don't wanna go. There're going to be thirty of the best-looking girls in New York, and a hundred and fifty guys in shirts and ties circling, hoping to strike; sharks going in for the kill—all your buddies who are worth millions and millions. What am I gonna do there?"

"Yeah, yeah," he said, and hung up.

Forty minutes later the intercom rang. It was Gino, the doorman. He said there was a big, long limousine down there, and they were waiting for me. Oh, well. I threw some velvets on, and a turtleneck, took my evening medicine of *two and two*—two sniffs of cocaine for each nostril—and jumped in the limo.

We headed over to West End Avenue. Obviously, Joel had had his medicine, too, because he was going a thousand words a minute, telling me about the women who were going to be there. We went up into a classic Art Deco building on 75th and Riverside where Ira Gershwin had lived many years before. As I'd expected, it looked like the Harvard Club, with a bunch of models, actresses, and movie star types, all beautifully dressed.

Well, I was committed, I was there; I made the most of it.

I looked around at the merchandise. The situation was exactly as I'd thought it would be: the statuesque beauties were being circled by suits and ties.

There was one tall girl who looked like a cross between a young Lauren Bacall and Bo Derek. She was wearing a green halter top and a white print skirt. She had great legs, a small waist, and the rest of her was right out of a magazine. She had long, blonde hair that left one beautiful green eye uncovered— like a screen goddess from the 1930s.

The hostess, Miss Delilah Henry, was not quite as tall, but she was elegant, sporting lots of gold jewelry and diamonds, and ordering around everyone in the kitchen. I got myself a plate of food and had a short conversation with Delilah, who I knew was Joel's friend. She was quite polite, and I asked her who that beauty was.

"It's an old friend who lives in the building." She looked at me shrewdly and added, "Barry, you really don't have a chance with that one. There are three millionaires waiting to marry her. Try another one."

I tried to make my move toward Diana Wilson. It was pretty difficult when there were five men surrounding her, moving in for the kill. I backed off and watched from the shadows. Then I saw my opening; they'd run out of champagne, and Diana announced she was going to get more.

I slid out the door as she left. I could see she was trying to ignore me. I was the only one not wearing a tie and a blue suit, so she might have thought I was the help. I introduced myself and asked if I might help her carry the champagne back to the party. We got in the elevator, and under the harsh lights she was even more gorgeous than I had thought.

My heart raced. I needed a plan. We went into her apartment, which was decorated beautifully, and in her living room she had a classic Turkmen rug from northern Afghanistan.

"Where did you get this rug?" I asked her.

"I got it from a guy who was just in a magazine. His name is Ivan."

"Well, what serendipity! He's my partner. That's half of my rug."

She laughed and I laughed, and now we had something in common.

We went back upstairs, and the party continued, but it was now getting late, and people were leaving. I asked her if she would like to go to a Halloween party two nights later, on Park Avenue. I told her a lot of interesting people would be there.

She told me that she was also invited to a party that night, and I could not possibly be invited to the same party. I knew it was a putdown, but I mentioned the name of the person giving the party, and, yes, it was the same.

I asked her if she would give me her number, and I would pick her up and take her there.

"Of course. I'm in the book. Diana Wilson, Riverside Drive."

But there was no Diana Wilson in the book. It was a lie.

I assembled my *Ocean's 11* crew, Jonathan, Jimmy, and Charlie, and told them that we were going to this party, and that I would point out a blonde who was very hard to miss, as she looked like Bo Derek.

"I want you guys not to let her talk to anybody else, and make sure that she constantly has a drink in her hand, and cocaine, if she needs it. Your job is to capture her. Rotate, keep her busy. You're doctors and lawyers; you'll figure it out. Just keep her busy."

•◊•◊•

I walked in, and saw her checking me out. I turned my head and pretended not to see her. I made my way over to the hostess and planted a juicy kiss on her lips and squeezed her ass. She was one of my old flames.

The place was full of models, Wall Street types, actors, lawyers, showgirls, garmentos, former ballplayers, and actors. It was getting to be about one o'clock, and my crew had done a magnificent job: Diana hardly got to talk to anyone else. And she was nice and high.

The party was breaking up, and they convinced her to go to Dr. Dollowicz's. I was already at the doctor's with two babes, waiting.

She came in with my four guys, the Doctor put his finest wares out on the table, and I nodded to her.

It was starting to get light out, and everyone was loaded.

I waited for her to move toward the elevator. My *Ocean's 11* crew disappeared.

I asked her if I could give her a cab ride home. She agreed. We jumped in the cab.

"Do you want to go home?" I asked.

"What is it you want to do at six o'clock in the morning?" she answered.

"Let's go to the Regency and have some breakfast. It's across the street from my apartment."

"Oh, that sounds great," she said.

When Diana came out of the bathroom, she was wearing my cotton Afghan shirt that was embroidered in Kandahar; today it's considered the most deadly place in Afghanistan, a Taliban stronghold. She had taken off her bra, and her figure, visible through the shirt, was more than I could ask for: there she was, statuesque, wondrously built, floating into my bedroom.

Our first kiss was not of this world—and I wasn't stoned, particularly since I had kept my wits about me in my efforts to try to entice her to my apartment. Her skin felt warm and inviting. I was intoxicated and spinning around. When we embraced, it actually felt like electricity was going through me. No amyl nitrate, no more drugs; it was real.

I had two postcards in my bathroom on 69th Street, and I loved them. They were given to me by an old friend, Andy Rhinestone, who ran *Midnight Blue,* the first X-rated TV show in New York. I framed them, and in my weird way, every time I would have a woman, or two women, I would look at these photographs and compare them to who was in my bed and say, "Nope, not yet."

But four hours after our first kiss, when I went into my bathroom, I looked at my beautiful pictures, and they seemed to be vibrating. I had to prop myself up because my head was still spinning.

We woke up a couple of days later. It was Sunday. Diana invited me to her house for brunch, and we spent a day in the park.

That evening, I found Diana's portfolio in the hallway, and I started looking through the pictures. Covers of *Cosmopolitan*, a lot of European publications, and great headshots. Toward the back of the book, I saw two framed art deco postcards, the face hidden with a masquerade mask and true '30s décor, identical to the ones in my bathroom.

"Who is in these postcards? That can't be you!"

"Yes, that's me. These postcards got an award," she said.

I froze, and I knew that was it. The hairs on the back of my neck stood up; I was flushed and got the chills.

And that was that. I had been saved by the bell.

We had a passionate and heated romance for three weeks. I could think of nobody but her from then on.

Usually, when women look like Diana and carry themselves the way she does, they're hard to get close to. Either they're terribly insecure—because they're so beautiful—or they're so narcissistic that they repel you. She had been brought up in Montana, in a wholesome way, and she was as good inside as she appeared on the outside. It was the perfect mixture for me— someone well read, highly intelligent, and beautiful.

After being with her for a few days, I lost my insatiable curiosity about other women, and forgot about conquest or chase. I was in a state of bliss; I felt complete.

Looking through her portfolio again while in her apartment one day, I found a copy of *Playboy* magazine from October, 1967 tucked way in the back, and discovered, much to my amazement, that she was the centerfold! She had never mentioned that...

I later learned that when Diana's grandparents found out about her being a *Playboy* Playmate centerfold, her grandfather, who always wore a shirt and tie, even when fishing, ran around in his '49 Ford buying every copy of *Playboy* he could get his hands on. I think he burned them all up for firewood. He didn't get all of them, though. After a while, he gave up, but he tried until his trunk filled up. But those were the '60s.

Diana had a modeling gig in Paris and didn't want to go. She wanted me to ask her to stay in America, but I wasn't sure she was sure. Even though I knew she was the one, part of me was still afraid of commitment. I wanted her to go off to see if she wanted me enough to come back. And I didn't want to be the one to end her acting and modeling career. I wanted it to be her own choice.

So off she went to Paris, and for the next week she kept calling me twice a day. And then three times a day.

Finally, I said, "Dear: One, this is getting terribly expensive. Two, come home."

"You mean it?"

"Yes, I'm sending you an Air France ticket."

I drove out to the airport to pick her up, so excited I was jumping around and looking for her. She tapped me on the shoulder after walking right past me. She was wearing a long, green Army coat and a French beret. I hadn't even recognized her. After spinning around , I tried not to look too embarrassed.

When it was time for me to meet her parents, I had to shave my beard and cut my hair to present the proper image of a solid citizen, and not a man of the night.

•◊•◊•

When I got off the plane in Missoula, Montana, all the men had long hair and beards. Boy, was I pissed!

Her family was wholesome and old-school—that is, conservative. Her grandma, whose house we stayed at, kept me trapped in the basement and stood guard.

As the weeks went by, I felt a quietness, a glow, and an inner peace. It grew stronger each day I was with Diana. My faculties began to return, and my loneliness and emptiness were filled. I no longer had any need to run. I could say whatever I wanted and so could she; neither of us was insecure about expressing our needs and opinions. For the first time, it was real conversation, with none of the neediness or play-acting or control issues that I had always had with women. I felt healed.

Kahlil Gibran's definition of a *friend* is "your needs answered," and I came to realize that this was truly what I had found in Diana. All of my needs were answered. I had found my other half, and she was my friend.

Chapter 17:

Santa Fe, Adobe, Ralph Lauren

When we got off the plane in Santa Fe in 1982, I thought we'd be there for a week, but we didn't leave for nearly three years.

Diana and I had decided to go to Santa Fe to pick up some cash and see what Ivan was up to. Ivan had a piece of property in downtown Santa Fe, an outdoor bazaar that he had rented for us, where he put rugs out every day. But he was doing only a little business. The problem was, he couldn't truck enough business down and do any volume selling because there was no place to store the stuff.

We settled in, in his guest room, and I forced him to rent the next building that had a little shop there. We filled it up with rugs. Within a year, we were very successful; we bought the building, and we were rocking. Money was pouring in. I was selling to Dallas Dopers, UFO people, and celebrities. I know Diana was getting lonely for New York, but it was a chance to make a big score.

The first week we were there, we went to the opening of the opera. Diana got dressed up beautifully, and if you looked quickly, she looked like Bo Derek, thank God for me. The next day people were asking me if I was dating Bo Derek. She caused quite a sensation with the hairy-legged set.

I was able to meet celebrities and robber barons without Francesca being the intermediary. They included John Connolly, Neil Simon, Marsha Mason, Billy Gibbons of ZZ-Top and Jack Nicholson.

Diana and I eloped to Las Vegas and got married in the Candlelight Chapel during our first year in Santa Fe, and I was able to tell my parents how well we were doing. I learned how to ski and bought real estate: my first house after Francesca. My parents came out and stayed at my place in Santa Fe. Diana gave them a traditional Passover Seder, and my father had tears in his eyes.

I had gone down on bended knee in the Spanish prison, and I had been given *shaktipat* by Muktananda, but this was the first time I felt spiritual without being under duress. In Santa Fe I met people who practiced the things I'd only studied and heard about.

They call Santa Fe a vortex. It ran the gamut of therapeutics. There were new-agers of every stripe, and considering the size of the town, there was also an abundance of traditional therapies— hypnosis, body work, psychodrama, art therapies. There was also a large inter-regional society of analysts who set up shop in the tradition of Swiss psychoanalyst Carl Jung. And there were Native American healers, *curanderas,* and practitioners of the cult of the green chili, one of New Mexico's unique contributions to world cuisine. You could find it all, day and night, as well as a large population of severely disturbed mentally ill, tended to by community mental health centers financed by Medicaid. There were the super-rich with their haciendas with great views on the road to the ski basin, and the poor with their trailer parks and run-down adobes.

But there was also a gathering of elements and folks from all over the world celebrating the idea that Santa Fe was a spiritual gathering place. There were spiritual bookstores: shops catering to those who followed Eastern religions with their concomitant texts and objects. There was a graduate school that specialized in courses in spiritual transformation; and there was the cachet of a town that carried a kind of light New Age ideology. To separate what was real and of the moment from what was simply New Age nonsense was the task of discerning minds. And indubitably, some of the New Age was really as old as the Sangre de Cristo Mountains that surrounded the town.

A group from Roswell said they had had abduction experiences. They said they felt like their brains had been put on tape recorders and their memories recorded. Three marks were put on their left breasts, and they were beamed back down. They reported being disoriented for weeks, months, or permanently.

On certain nights when the sky was very clear, they felt they were taken out of their beds, levitated, and lifted back up to these vehicles. Many described bright rooms, medical procedures, shiny stainless steel, glass, and high frequencies. My friend, Reba, had three very strange marks on her chest and claimed to be in this group.

I went to a dinner party where there was a young couple with very light eyes and quirky personalities. They walked as if their feet weren't even touching the floor, and claimed they were from another planet. They did a Q and A, and there was a group there from Los Alamos asking questions over my head about molecular matter and Einstein's theories, but nobody was laughing at them. The next day I went over to see them, but they were gone. They were the talk of the town for the next couple of weeks. In retrospect, they did not appear real, because their skin was too translucent and their veins too blue.

I had past-life regressions, several guided by psychologists. Everybody seemed to be going to find out who they were, where they came from, and where they were going.

One of my past lives was apparently Biblical—I was with the moneychangers on the day Jesus showed up at the temple, and he knocked over one of my tables after I had cheated Ivan out of all of his money. My karmic debt to Ivan was apparently repaid in this life. I was one of *them*—the hypocrites. I sold doves and holy objects and took money, so Jesus knocked my table over and screamed at me and shamed me that day. I described the streets, and everything that was going on. When I woke up and listened to the tape, I didn't quite believe it. I still don't.

In another regression, I was with Joshua, and was allowed to go to the Promised Land and carry his ram's horn. Then I was Samuel, a merchant who came over from the old country, and lived out near the Hamptons, never married, and did a lot of charity work. That was at the turn of the century. The only one I got a kick out of was the moneychangers story, because it all made sense. And I've always felt close to the Biblical times in my travels through the Middle East and Central Asia. I often felt as if I carried within myself some kind of archetypal experience of the ancient world.

Ralph Lauren came through town one day when Ivan and I were in litigation over some rug business. I was eating lunch up on Canyon Road, and he came by with his entourage and bought blankets, handicrafts, and prairie skirts—he cleaned the town out. I understand that his photographers shot all the architecture. We did not exchange words or looks—he was just a whirlwind. He later bought loads of rugs from Ivan for all the Ralph Lauren stores. And that gave Ivan a huge boost.

Our shop was right downtown in the main square, in a big open courtyard. Everybody had to walk through there on the way to the opera or dinner, right by the creek that flowed through Santa Fe, on Alameda and Shelby. We planned to stay only a week or so on our way back to New York from Montana, and it became three years. We got caught up in the swirl—and the black hole.

First of all, you can get sick of an adobe, because everything looks the same. The architecture is very beautiful, the streets are charming, the shops are wonderful, but give me a break. How much mud could I look at?

I got my first taste there of *Texas hospitality* and real Texans. I had had a good experience with Mrs. Yost from American Airlines in New York, where I had also once spent a wonderful afternoon with the Basses who hailed from Fort Worth. They were impressive, elegant people. But this new group was from Midland, Bartlesville, Wichita Falls, and they wore the gear: the Stetson, the boots, the big belts, the tight jeans, with those gold American Express cards to match their Rolexes. They were good ol' boys.

I got along with them, and they were great. They had a sense of humor, they were crazy about sports, they told long stories, and their wives came on Saturdays or Sundays, when they were watching the games, and spent big money.

The Sufi Nation was there, and their leader, Pierre Valaya Khan. He had a house up in the mountains with his charming wife, and his son, who worked for me. He was a trip, and so was his secretary, and his business manager, the Shanazz. He was a real sharpie and a good guy. We became close friends.

Up in Abiquiu, they had a monastery run by Neradine, a six-five, redheaded spiritualist. He exuded great power, and was involved in building a beautiful retreat up there for the Sufis.

We were loaded with spiritual energy. There were other groups with many wives like Mormons, wearing robes. They were into business. There were sheiks, and, of course, the Catholic Church. There were Pueblo Indians down at the square in Santa Fe, who were still suffering from the slaughter of their forefathers in the 15th century. Many of the men hung out on corners, drinking hooch, and asking for money.

The indigenous Chicano population was at odds with the Indians. I didn't know it at the time, but Santa Fe was the rape capital of America. I was there when they had the prison riots, and many people were killed in the uprising.

There was also a group that would go back and forth from Sedona and swear that they'd been in flying saucers. They had weekend meetings at various homes to introduce Space People, and they were dead serious. They would come with "proof"— those marks on their breasts when they were operated on in spaceships. I went to quite a few of them—I was curious. Some of these people had the strangest eyes and coloring. It was *The X-Files* before *The X-Files*. There was no Scully or Mulder yet, but there were plenty of these people around.

There was weekend chanting from the Sufis, meetings of MUFON—the Mutual UFO Network—Indian dances, low riders driving around town all night causing trouble, highbrow operas, chamber music, drunks, and the line on the first of the month was huge at the post office. Yes, it was a trust fund town. They didn't earn the money; it was earned generations back.

There was also a contingent of Afghan refugees. Mabuba, the niece of the assassinated President Dahud, lived there, too. We had a nice melting pot of different ethnic groups and religions.

I found it fascinating, but I was getting allergic to adobe and *faralitos*, which are little lighted candles in bags; there are thousands all over the city during Christmas. It was very beautiful—at least for one Christmas.

I will say this for Ivan: for all his lack of sophistication, he did intuitively have the most incredible taste. He could combine colors and match things that looked as if they wouldn't work, and make them perfect. He really had the eye. And he taught me how to do it. He shared with me his knowledge of how to pick and choose and acquire the best pieces. I am indebted to him for doing that. He left me with a terrific toolset for earning money working with decorators later in life. Now all I need is a little piece of fabric, and I can match it perfectly.

And I did get to meet a lot of interesting people back then. Don Meredith, from *Monday Night Football*, lived in Santa Fe, and we became buddies. When I'd be traveling to Dallas, we shared a lot of stories. He had a hell of a sense of humor and was a good guy. He sent a lot of his "good ol' boy" friends over to buy rugs, and everybody walked through that yard, from John Connolly to Neil Simon and Marsha Mason. They were all customers.

When the first winter came, it got very cold, and the town emptied. Our business dropped 90 percent, so we decided to load a truck full of our best merchandise and see if we could sell it on the road. Everybody was talking about this town in Colorado, where all the movie stars were and all the money was—Aspen.

We drove the truck up through the back country, came out through Colorado Springs, into Denver, and took the highway toward Aspen. It was snowing like a bitch. I could barely see, and it took us hours to get down, as the Eisenhower Pass had been closed. Finally, we got into Aspen and rented out the back room of the old Jerome Hotel.

I flew my kids in, figuring we'd all do some skiing, I'd do some selling, and we'd all have a good time.

The town was dazzling and loaded with pretty people. The kids told me who they were, but since I didn't care which movie stars were which, it really didn't matter. I was there for the money.

The first day was great. We made a lot of money, and I made a big sale to a character who looked like he was a grandpa, with black glasses and a long red beard. He gave me a gold card and bought a whole bunch of rugs—and got me stoned. He told me his name was Billy Gibbons, and that his group was ZZ Top. That night, they made so much noise jamming down the hall that Diana screamed so loudly that they either went to sleep or moved to other rooms.

The next day, the kids and I went skiing, and there was a Jack Nicholson sighting. My son, Tony, loved him. He drove by in his black Range Rover with his black shirt and black glasses. That night we were in the Jerome Bar, and he walked in with his entourage. He was magnetic, and he lit the room up—and the party started. I was in the back working with some customers when he walked in and tripped over some rugs. I think he'd had a few drinks. Tony spoke with him, and then Jack decided to sleep there for a while.

After another year in Santa Fe, the rug wars continued. We were selling so cheap that the other dealers were complaining and moving out of town to Taos. *Architectural Digest* did a story about the shop, and interior design magazines made us a must-see in Santa Fe.

After three years in Santa Fe, I couldn't stand the adobe or Ivan anymore, even though we were making so much money. So we parted ways.

Chapter 18:

Dallas Does Dope

Before Ivan and I split up, we were offered a joint venture by the RTMark Company on Highland Drive right next to the Design Center. The owner had a great showroom, a good reputation, and a strange name—Mark Bustboom. We sold him a truckload of rugs for his Dallas showroom, and part of the deal was that I would help set it up and monitor the cash flow.

I did most of the work with our Dallas partner. I would leave Santa Fe on Mondays and come back on Fridays. The rug trade in Dallas was booming. We put rugs out on a friend's lawn priced at twenty grand, and people would buy them up. When my partnership with Ivan finally dissolved, I moved to Dallas full-time.

The people in Dallas knew how to dress: the men very East Coast, in beautifully tailored suits, the women right out of Neiman Marcus, Saks Fifth Avenue, and Chanel. People took their time with what they wore, coordinated it all, and their lives revolved around entertaining, dinner parties, and the national pastime: drinking. They were two-fisted professionals—male and female.

They had unusual rules there. You could drive with an open can or a drink in your hand with a gun or rifle in the back seat of your pickup truck. This led to a lot of signs with holes in them.

The good ol' boys would get all fired up and take a few shots on the way home. I found it disconcerting that they were mixing cocktails and driving at excessive speeds, with no seatbelts and a truck full of weapons.

It was a very seductive time. As in New York, everybody had their vial of coke, and the disco biscuits were easy to get in Dallas, also.

They had the showroom ready, and the party started at five o'clock, when the beer, and the booze, and the wine, and the blow would all come out.

There were huge hotels, and mansions owned by people like the Hunts, great little bars like the Stoneleigh Pea, and the Wine Press on Oak Lawn. Since my partner, Mark, "the Boomer," lived there, he knew everybody. He had a nice house on Oak Lawn, and gave me the keys because he was about to get married to Miss Ginger on Highland Park.

At that time, I caught my first up-close glimpse of AIDS. Jim, one of the salesmen in our showroom, a real nice guy, was losing five pounds a week, and it was early in the epidemic. It was hard for us to understand. But after a month, we knew. The blotches came out. It was terrifying. He was handsome, virile, and an athlete, but he turned into a skeleton before our eyes.

The design business is like the entertainment business— filled with people who are gay and bisexual—so it was scaring the hell out of everyone. Every showroom seemed to have somebody who was losing weight. It *was* an epidemic; so many emaciated men with blotches on their faces, and nobody understood what was going on.

Next to the Design Center was Cedar Springs, the gay section of Dallas. The foreshadowing was all over the walls. The end of time was coming. Pestilence was upon us.

I started flying in on Mondays, on the old Southwest Airlines, from Albuquerque.

At first, I stayed in a lot of nondescript hotels around Stemmons Avenue near the Design Center. I would work with my new partner, the Boomer, with his big white head of hair and his little moustache and his little chuckle. He looked like the poor man's Clark Gable, with blond hair.

We convinced the Boomer to give us a bunch of money and

buy some rugs and put them in his huge showroom on Highland Drive.

The Boomer's showroom had a big front for showing and a rear for receiving. We took over the rear. The girls all dressed, the guys wore jeans and work shirts. Dallas was in full bloom, and I was sitting pretty.

We had all the high rollers, and the top designers would come in. The first big sale was to the owner of Billy Bob's from Fort Worth. They kept coming. The Murchisons, the Basses, Ross Perot Jr., Trample Crow—on and on, and the money poured in.

So did the drugs and the alcohol. We hung out in the new Rosewood Hotel. Jean Street owned a chain of soul food restaurants called the Black-Eyed Peas. There I met my soul brother, David Bell, whose family adopted me. My first day there, he took me out to trade, and I got myself a couple of pairs of cowboy boots so I could be a shit-kicker just like the rest of them.

David had season tickets to the Maverick games, and he introduced me to the public relations woman, who became a friend. I had a seat at the end of the bench at most of the games. I was stylin'.

I didn't have a car yet, so I used the white cargo van. It was kind of odd riding around in it when everybody else had Beamers, Mercedes, and Rollses.

Miss Ginger, the Boomer's fiancée, talked him into moving to Houston; that would be his downfall, and I would crash with it. Everyone advised against it because it was too much overhead, but he overextended himself, opening up a second showroom in Houston.

Then, the banks started going under, one at a time. People put their oil wells up as collateral. Oil started moving down—from thirty dollars a barrel to twelve. The boom was over. If the Boomer hadn't opened up his second showroom—expanding into Houston at the worst possible time, when all the trouble was going on—we would have been able to weather the storm. But the auctioneer arrived, and the keys were handed over.

I was forced to move to Oak Lawn, to a beautiful 3,000-square-foot place. The men who leased it to me were a team of real estate guys: they all had matching Beamers, and so did their wives. They had been making a lot of money in real estate, flipping buildings with mortgages.

There were six partners, and they were very classy guys, fixtures in Dallas society. They would go to the bars at five o'clock for business meetings, and this would go on with hours of drinking, dining, and sports events. They discussed where they bought their shoes, which tailors they went to, and where they got their ties. They were prosperous and frivolous—it was never going to end, they had oil, they were Dallas—and they really did believe that Texas was a separate country from the rest of the United States.

They were loud, good ol' boys who could always be found late at night in the clubs. They loved to eat, drink, tell filthy jokes, slap each other on the back, and give each other cigars. I loved them; you could make a deal with them. They were into honor and shaking hands, even though they were drunk and doped out.

I only knew the rich ones then. I didn't know about the down-and-out characters because I wasn't roaming the city at night anymore—I was staying at the best hotels, drinking the finest champagnes. Diana and I had dinner with them a lot, and they treated me as an equal.

There was no business going on, so I couldn't pay rent, and one of the owners of the building, let's call him C. Martin III, was smart enough to barter with me, seeing that it was a strategic way to do business. Many of his renters could not afford to pay the rent when the economy slid, so he decided he might as well take products from them—otherwise he'd lose all his buildings. I started giving him so many rugs that he opened an antique store in one of his shopping malls. I couldn't pay rent, but I sure had rugs.

Through some attorneys I knew, who were into barter, I was able to trade rugs for BMWs and Mercedes, Piaget watches, all kinds of high-end clothes for Diana, diamond rings, cases of fine wine, and tickets to Cowboy games. It was like a bazaar.

We were sniffing and drinking. Fortunately, I was married and didn't chase trim anymore.

But we were enduring great stress because there was no money coming in.

The *For Sale* signs went out and the moving trucks came; people were heading to New York, to Chicago, to Miami, and L.A.

The banks folded. That was it, Dallas was done. And then the stock market dropped eight hundred points. They remortgaged to get out of the hole using real estate investment trusts, which propped up the banks and eventually straightened out the whole mess, but it took Dallas ten years to recover.

•◊•◊•

I knew California was still booming because I'd made several buying and selling trips there. So I flew out there to try and do some business and stayed with Rodney, my friend from Long Island, who was now a hack writer and a quasi-agent—one of his clients had a hit TV series. Rodney had a Rolls-Royce, a Mercedes, five motorcycles, twenty motorcycle jackets, fifteen Armani suits, and no cash.

On the way back to Dallas, I took an excursion to Phoenix, and the next thing I knew I was with the Space People in Sedona. Sleeping on top of the coffee pot vortex, staying up for days looking for flying saucers with Reba with the marked chest, and I wasn't even high. I did have a propensity for magnetizing unusual people to me.

They showed me where they found the UFOs, and Tesla had set up experiments. The people in Sedona always looked weird to me. Clearly, Sedona was not an option.

When I returned to Dallas, Diana was ready to leave. She had had enough of Dallas and the heat. It was time to go back to the ocean, since she'd grown up in Santa Monica.

We loaded everything we'd collected in Dallas into a huge moving truck, hooked up the Mercedes Lapis, and drove the BMW to L.A., to our new house on Holloway.

I said goodbye to the condo, said goodbye to RTMark, the sniff, the whiff, the coke, the smoke, the gin, the vodka... It really was time to get out of there.

Chapter 19:

Coldwater Canyon, Celebrity Avenue

It was the early '80s. I was staying in the old Holiday Inn on Highland Avenue. We were transitioning and still living in Dallas. I had some rugs in a tiny antique store in Woodland Hills, and I was trying to test the market. I was bored, so I picked some rugs up and walked down Highland, near Hollywood High School, and threw them over the fence.

I met the weirdest people on Hollywood and Vine: panhandlers, grifters, entertainment types on the way to work in their Beamers, and people dressed in Frederick's of Hollywood costumes in the middle of the afternoon—and it felt like being on 42nd Street in New York. It's an iconic corner. These people started pulling over and giving me cash for these rugs. Before I knew it, they were all gone. I went back to the hotel and said, "Damn! This city is lined with gold!"

I flew back to Dallas, and arranged a caravan that left Dallas with one moving truck full of furniture, antique rugs, and household possessions. Behind that, our Mercedes Lapis was being pulled by Salvador Sanchez from the State of Jalisco in Mexico. Behind him, I was in my Ford Econoline van loaded with household items, my shotgun, and various collectibles.

It took us almost three days to get there. My gray BMW was

already in the garage, safe. I had rented a house at 8737 Holloway Drive, backed up to Nicky Blair's restaurant and right off the Sunset Strip. It was a 1930s cottage with a pleasant backyard.

I'd left another showroom open in Dallas and sent Mr. Sanchez back to run it, while I was hoping to prospect for gold in the Hollywood Hills.

The neighborhood was alive. There were actors, waiters, car attendants, and others in the entertainment business. The street rocked on the weekends.

We had cards made and started trying to sell to interior designers and the public. I wasn't sure what to do with my time because I couldn't tell if it was winter, summer, or fall: it was the same every day. Everybody appeared to be rich, and to have a brand new car.

Also in the mix were guys from Iran. Middle Easterners seemed to be all over Beverly Hills and Truesdale, and I heard Farsi spoken on every street corner.

La Cienega was right around the corner, so I could go every day and drink sweet tea and hunt around for rugs and antiques. Spago was in my back yard, and the Ivy was just around the block.

We sold the rugs out of the house, and were holding our own. One day, I was driving up Coldwater Canyon, and I saw two men selling cactus and mirrors on the side of the road, right where Coldwater cuts into Mulholland, across from the Tree People's Park.

I liked this mountain, so I set up my office there. I had a whole house full of antique rugs, and I had a blue Mercedes Lapis with Dallas plates that said *WOVEN1*.

I set up on the side of the road and put my rugs out by Ray, the cactus man, from New Orleans and Ben, selling mirrors. Ben was a tennis pro, but he sold mirrors part-time—tennis must have been a poor career choice. The three of us set up camp; a little cactus, a few mirrors, and a helluva lot of rugs.

So there I was, with our rugs out on the Road to the Stars, and they came. My first sales to celebrities were to Laura Dern and young Heather Locklear.

•◊•◊•

Weenie was living up in Topanga, and I had stayed at his house for a week before Diana came out with the caravan and while our house was being renovated. We never talked about jail or Mr. Red-Eyes, but he accommodated me. He had his ex-wife living in the house, along with a girlfriend in another room. He was up to the old spiritual game. Diana was still back in Texas packing up the house.

Weenie had pictures of Muktananda all over the walls. He was making lotions and concoctions in the garage, with jojoba oil, teatree oil, and all sorts of holistic herbs. His restaurant was sold to some Koreans who had a health food store, and the real estate that he owned in the middle of town was sold to the Carlsons, who later became my best friends in Topanga for years. The karma was running pretty good.

I later passed by one of the properties, which is now called Topanga Home Grown. It was a converted railroad caboose with a bunch of vegetables out front.

Our next-door neighbor in Hollywood was Nicky Blair, who had the Nicky Blair restaurant, one of the celebrity landmarks. His roommate was Bernie Schwartz, from the Bronx, also known as Tony Curtis, whom I later got to visit with at the Playboy mansion. Nicky also knew Dr. Dollowicz from Brooklyn, and when I finally found the Doctor to say goodbye, he sent Nicky his regards from Broadway.

The first Playboy party I attended was in 1983. It was our first year back in L.A. and I was living in West Hollywood when we received our invitation to one of Hef's annual *Midsummer Night's Dream* parties. Diana talked about it excitedly for days— who was going to be there, and so on. My attitude was more like, "Okay, I'm ready!"

We discussed the dress code, which meant lingerie for her and pajamas for me. I had trouble believing that we would drive up to the Playboy mansion and everybody else would actually be dressed that way. To me, a suspicious, streetwise New Yorker, it felt like a hoax. And what if I got pulled over by a cop and he asked me to get out and I was in my pajamas and a robe and

Diana was in lingerie? Anyway, where was I going to put my wallet and money?

After some discussion, we did it anyway. I was game.

On the evening of the party, we got to the mansion and drove up the long driveway. In those days, they didn't have the security that they have today, with the shuttle buses and the checkpoints. The valet took my blue Mercedes off our hands and we joined a line of pajama and lingerie-clad revelers. The dress code was clearly being honored by all.

I remember walking through the door of Hef's place, and noticing on the left a painting of Dalí's melting clocks, one of the series. Hef certainly had taste.

We went into the vestibule, and Diana knew all the girls. There were hugs and kisses, a lot of handshaking with other husbands and dates. Then we moved into the main area where the party always took place, the back yard of his estate, which was covered with a massive tent. There were no chairs or tables, just enormous cushions and very low stands for food and drink.

I sat down on the floor and could not believe where I was. The most beautiful women in the world, celebrities galore, music... I believe it was Ray Anthony's band.

The food was sumptuous—steaks, lobsters, everything imaginable.

Some of Diana's Playmate friends came over. Barbi Benton, Hef's ex, came and sat with us, unassuming and fun. And before I knew it there were five or six beautiful Playmates with their husbands and dates hanging out with us. They laughed and talked mainly about the old days, when they lived at the mansion and worked for Playboy in various capacities. The ladies talked about who was going to Glamourcon that year. (Glamourcon is an annual event where dozens of Playmates greet collectors and autograph copies of the magazine.)

After a while I wandered off and had conversations with Tony Curtis, Robert Culp (the actor), and football Hall-of-Famer Jim Brown. I tried to talk to Kareem Abdul Jabbar, but he was flowing by in his white robes, very impressive at seven-four, and I couldn't quite catch up with him.

I was urged to sit down at a long table with eight beautiful women and this large, imposing man at the end. "Go sit with him," several people told me. "There's plenty of room!" I sat down to visit, and the man literally growled at me. It turned out he was Jerry Buss, the owner of the Lakers, and it was an inside joke that you never sat at his table. They were laughing at me, I was set up!

People were very comfortable, and it felt like a pleasant family gathering. Security was pervasive but not obvious, and there were no incidents. Considering the amount of alcohol that was consumed, the guests were quite well behaved. It was a love-in without any lovemaking, at least no hanky-panky that I could see. I made a point of checking out the famous grotto, which was open to all. I had no idea what was going on upstairs in the mansion, however. People were always going in and out...

By the time we left, I felt privileged to have been allowed to hang out with a very interesting group of people, who welcomed me warmly as if I'd been there before, even though I was really just a rookie.

We had arrived around nine-thirty and left probably at one, when it was just starting to get hot. People were coming from other parties. I'd say there were well over a thousand people there, as opposed to 2014, when the New Year's Eve party that we attended hosted only about two hundred or so of Hef's closest friends.

Probably the most dramatic event that I witnessed at a Playboy party was the arrival of Anna Nicole Smith at the Halloween bash in 2004. There was huge buzz going around and everybody was trying to outdo everybody else, when all of a sudden there was a roar in the room and it opened up like the red sea. A ravishing woman came down the aisle with a three-foot hat on and a pink and purple outfit, giving off electricity. Everybody held their breath and moved back. She took over the room, embraced Hef, and said hello to the girls. Then she drifted out onto the dance floor. Later, like Cinderella, she disappeared.

It was an interesting experience to be the husband of a Playboy Playmate, because when you walked into an event where you were sort of an appendage of another person, you wound up being put with others, mainly husbands, who were similar. You really had no identity. Many of these husbands were very powerful men in commerce and entertainment, but in the Playboy environment, nobody cared about them. They were used to lifting a finger and making and breaking careers, and here their wives were the royalty. They had to get up and get their own food.

Quite often I would never be formally introduced to these men; when other Playmates came over, we were just *them*. The Playmates would just nod at us. It was almost like high school.

I've watched these guys get gray and chunky and lose their hair over the years, and some of them finally divorced. Some went missing or were replaced by another husband.

You had to prepare yourself for this. As the years went on, I frequently found myself wanting to leave these parties after just a few hours, even though I was having a great time. It could wear you down, the fact that you didn't have a name and you had to fill time and be very conscious of your wife and not get too lost, which was very easy there.

Also, still having occasional flashbacks from my old days at Studio 54 and the Botany Club, I always had to be a little careful not to be tempted when I had a little too much time on my hands.

As Diana and I continued to attend the parties over the years, we got to where we always seemed to separate as soon as we walked into the mansion. She would run and grab her girlfriends from so many years back who came from all over the world for this event. Young women would approach me and ask if I was a producer or could get them into a movie. Little did they know I was lucky to get into the men's room. I had no pull in that direction. But looks can be deceiving; I had a black tie on and was starting to get a little silver fox-looking.

And sometime during the evening I'd see this gorgeous five-foot-ten blonde with an incredible body go past me. I was about to say "Wow!"—and then I'd realize that was my wife.

Diana always complained that I never danced with her at these events, but I'm just not a natural dancer like she is.

For some reason, at many of the parties I attended at the mansion, whenever I was dancing I seemed to trip over Bill Maher's shoes. It always happened. And I would have to say, he was with the best-looking girls at every party. We would then visit a bit, say hello and goodbye. I'm sure he didn't know my name, but it was fun just hanging out for a few minutes.

I didn't attend one of the Halloween parties in the early 2000s, but my wife and her best friend, Nancy Harwood, were at the big bar standing next to George Clooney and the great character actor Ed Lauter. George was his charming self, and visited with Nancy and Diana. Lauter also got into a conversation with Diana. He mentioned that he was from Long Island, and she mentioned that her husband was also from Long Island. Of course it was the same hometown, Long Beach, Long Island, where I'm from.

"What's his name?" Lauter asked.

"Barry Hornig," she said.

"The pole vaulter?"

"Yes! Do you know him?"

"You know how many times we had beer together and he watched me play football and I watched him play basketball? Where is he?"

That started my relationship with Eddie Lauter over the following decade. He was in 150 movies. Alfred Hitchcock said he was one of our great character actors. He was the bald guard in *The Longest Yard* who was forever fighting with Burt Reynolds. He was generous and kind, and did everything he could to help me with my screenplays. May he rest in peace.

At the New Year's Eve party going into 2015, the ceiling opened, the balloons fell out, and Ray Anthony tried to blow his horn. He was old and a little tired, but he did it. Happy New Year! I grabbed my wife and gave her a passionate kiss. Her body was warm and inviting. I was aroused. I was the luckiest man in the world. Here I was at the best party that anyone could want—with my soulmate. And here came the New Year.

But it was a relatively small event. Hef had only about 200 people. It was his close friends, poker buddies, Playmates and husbands, and some Playboy executives who'd been with him for years.

Lauter wasn't there that year, and was greatly missed.

Robert Culp wasn't there; he'd also passed on. It had always been good to sit down with him and talk with him about his adventures. He was articulate and kind, full of great stories.

Bernie Schwartz (Tony Curtis) also wasn't there anymore. He'd always had a good tale or two about the Bronx, and about his ex-roommate, Nicky Blair (my neighbor). And he still had his great New York accent.

And there was no more driving up in your car like the old days. You'd go on a secure bus, and they'd cut your wristband off before you got back on the bus to leave.

One evening two weeks after my first Playboy party, Diana was walking Huey, our very smart, very kind, and very unaggressive lab shepherd, down the Sunset Strip, when a man came out of the shadows and walked toward them in a menacing way. Huey bit the man in the leg and ripped his leather pants. He started screaming, "Police! Police! Arrest that dog!" Diana and Huey took off around the corner. The madman gave chase. They ran into the back of Nicky Blair's restaurant, which was full of people. They told Nicky they were on the lam and being chased. Nicky said, "Don't worry about a thing; we'll hide you guys in the refrigerator!" The maniac came into the place and started dropping names, screaming that he was going to have the dog killed. They asked him politely to leave before they had him arrested. They opened the refrigerator and gave Huey a bone and Diana a steak dinner.

After that, Nicky opened up a big restaurant in Vegas. He recently died, but he was a real Damon Runyan character. His bedroom was right across from mine on Holloway. The man certainly had a great sex drive. Two or three times a week he would have a different woman in his house. It was always the same: "Come on up, we'll have a drink. Nicky'll show you how to get to heaven." I would chuckle and fall asleep, or be awakened and smother a laugh. And they would scream, "Nicky! You're taking me to Paradise! You're taking me to Paradise!" Or sometimes they would leave: Heaven wasn't open that night.

Just as we were getting a foothold in Hollywood, Iraq moved into Kuwait, which started the First Gulf War. And that immediately brought the recession to L.A. in full force. We weren't getting our designers, and the citizens weren't coming to the house to buy rugs. All the shops had *For Sale* signs in the windows. Melrose Avenue did not have the traffic, and I was getting worried. Dallas all over again.

We had settled our legal dispute with Ivan, got chump change, sold our house in Santa Fe at the wrong time, and we had to let our condo go in Dallas, so our staying power was weak. I had too much inventory because nobody wanted it.

I had to come up with a plan.

I didn't want to rent a shop and create overhead or be a merchant. I didn't want to give anybody merchandise on consignment. With the weak economy, I was worried about being ripped off.

We drove out to Paradise Cove one Saturday afternoon to have some lunch. At Trancas, on the side of the road, were people selling fresh fish, shrimp, jeans, oil paintings, and more cactus. Cars pulled up with people who had money to burn. This was on the cliff at the top right, below Broad Beach, where Michael Eisner, Stallone, Spielberg, and the other powerhouses lived. It was a heavily-traveled road.

The next weekend, I loaded up my van, picked a day worker up on the corner, and drove out to the beach. In Dallas, when we were trying to get out of town, we went into vacant gas stations and hung up rugs and fancy Neiman Marcus bags that sold for two hundred each. We'd come home after the weekend with a pocketful of cash. I figured if it worked there and in the bazaar in the Middle East, and all over the world, it sure could work in Malibu with the Big Rich. That weekend, I sold two or three rugs to some locals, and they asked me when I'd be back, as they had friends who also needed rugs. A nice Jewish doctor showed up, an anesthesiologist at Cedars. He said he was a rug collector and asked if I would come to his house and take a look. He lived in Point Dune in a castle on the bluffs, wedged in between Bob Dylan and Johnny Carson. He had a few nice pieces and good taste. He was from New York, a good guy. I sold him half a dozen rugs, and then a friend of his came over and bought a few more. My overhead was gasoline, a day worker, and some sandwiches. Everyone else around me was selling merchandise, cars were pulling over, people were screeching, and I felt that this was too good to last because someone would get into an accident or something inexplicable would happen on the side of the road. But I plugged along for a few more weekends and made some more money.

I started going out on occasional Fridays, too, to get ready for the weekend. One beautiful Friday, when I was sitting looking out at the ocean, a black BMW pulled up. An older guy got out, close to age sixty, long hair, and jeans spattered with paint. He said his name was Herb Alpert. He told me he was doing a favor for a dear friend of his who was very sick, and wasn't going to be around much longer. He was giving him one of his houses in Malibu, up on the mountain, and he was furnishing the house for him. They were working on music together, and he wanted to give him some dignity before he died. I was deeply touched. Then he told me it was Stan Getz that he was doing it for.

He told me that Stan was going to be coming over to look at some of the rugs, and not to worry about the money, just to give him what he wanted.

Stan came by later and picked out a group of Sumac rugs from Armenia. He said they reminded him of musical notes. I followed him up to his house, and Herb was there. As we visited, he laid the rugs out, and I saw that the whole fireplace had been done as a collage of old saxophones. He gave me a copy of the new album he'd just made with Herb.

Later, he came back down and we went back to the house. He took out his sax and meandered about, playing a few songs. He talked about the old days, Coltrane and Miles and all the hipsters. The afternoon drifted by. I put the tape on as I drove home, thinking how lucky I was to meet him.

The police finally moved in and asked everybody to get out of there or be locked up. Everybody scattered. I moved down the beach a little to Kanan Dune, where there was a vacant lot. I came back the following Friday and set up. I was reading a book when Ron Wilson, one of the top designers in Los Angeles, pulled up and said, "I love these rugs. We're gonna slice 'em up and make furniture cushions, and they're gonna go to Cher's house in Aspen." I thought to myself, *If he wants to destroy those beautiful weavings it makes me sick, but even if he wants to cook them and make chop suey out of them, that's okay with me; I need the money.*

I lasted another month on that corner, cash flowing in, until I noticed too many police cars noticing me. It was time to move my circus.

One day, out of curiosity, I drove back up to my original street selling spot on Coldwater near the Tree People Park. I noticed a small green area and a phone booth. I drove by and saw somebody selling bonsai plants close by. I guess Ray and Ben had moved on.

Up went the blue truck, out came the rugs. I put them on the fence that was backed up on a home. The next day an old man came out and said, "What are you doing with that stuff on my fence?" I said, "I'm trying to get a hip replacement, and I need to make some money." He laughed at me and said, "Come in the house, I need a rug. Call me Kirsch."

He had *Star Wars* posters on the walls and plaques for directing and Emmys. He sat down and we visited. When I asked him about the awards, he said, "Yeah, I had a little to do with *Star Wars.*" He turned out to be Irwin Kirschner, who had directed *The Empire Strikes Back.*

I said, "Here, Kirsch, take one of these rugs, and let me use your fence."

"Okay, sounds like a good deal."

On my second week there, about two in the afternoon, a car came dangerously close to me and skidded to a stop in front of the rugs hanging there. A tall girl in tight jeans got out with no makeup on. She started walking around my display. She told me she had just bought a house around the corner and needed rugs. She picked one of them up, asked me the price, and set it aside. This went on for about an hour, as she made a pile. We went through it; she started driving the price down, and I kept driving it up again. Finally, she kicked the pile and asked, "Do you wanna sell 'em, or do you wanna leave 'em here lying in the dirt?"

I couldn't help it; I fell on the ground and started laughing.

"What's so damned funny?" she demanded.

"Lady, I don't know who you are, but you must be an actress. This is ridiculous."

She laughed and wrote me a check. We had a laughing goodbye, a peck on the cheek, and an embrace.

"Thank you, I had a good time," she said.

"Thank you, I had a great time."

That was the first of several meetings I had with my on-and-off buddy, Sharon Stone.

The next weekend, it got really crowded up there. A skinny kid with little granny glasses and ripped-up jeans came down on a motorcycle and picked out a nice assortment of rugs from Turkey, and said he'd be back in a little while. He came back in a truck and said, "Lemme try them." He had an English accent. I said, "Go for it."

He came back a few hours later without the rugs, and sat down on the beach chair next to me. We started talking about New York, and he mentioned that he was in the music business. He thanked me and asked, "Is it okay if I give you a check? I don't have this much cash in the house. I live right up on Mulholland." I said, "Okay." I looked at the check. It had three or four attorneys' names, in care of Julian Lennon, John's son.

Fifteen minutes later, an antique convertible pulled up, driven by a guy honking the horn like Clarabelle. He had a huge chin and a leather jacket. He looked at the rugs, we had a little visit, and he made me laugh. The next day he drove by in another old car, and waved to me. That afternoon, he pulled up in another antique car. Finally, I figured out that he was Jay Leno. I didn't watch much TV at the time.

One afternoon, an intellectual old Jew came by in a brand new Jaguar with two beautiful dogs in the back seat. He looked at the rugs, put some in the trunk, and told me he'd be back with his girlfriend. His name was Daniel Melnick, and he was in the entertainment business. He was actually quite hot at that time, producing some big movies with Mario Kassar. He gave me his card, and came back with his girlfriend, Lisa. They picked out some more rugs. He told me he was making a few movies, and he was in the Tower Building, with a big art collection.

"People say I'm crazy, but I'm really not," he said.

Melnick played cards with Johnny Carson once a week, and his girlfriend was writing for *Buzz* magazine, which was brand new at the time. She picked out one rug for herself, and asked me how I wound up on this mountain with all these beautiful rugs. I told her my story; she asked me if I'd like to be in a feature article in a new magazine.

"Why would anyone be interested in reading about a rug dealer on top of a mountain?"

She said because I was selling to all those celebrities, and people would be interested.

I thought she was just blowing smoke up my ass. But a week later, a photographer from *Buzz* magazine came by and said he wanted to photograph me at my house with the rugs. I said, "Okay, why not?"

When the magazine came out, Laura Dern was on the cover, and there was a two-page story about me selling rugs at Coldwater Canyon. After the magazine article appeared, they started to come: lawyers, doctors, celebrities.

But soon, there were a couple of car accidents up on the corner and complaints from the neighbors. It was time to fold my tent.

I moved my circus over to Laurel Canyon, across from Houdini's old house, where a bunch of old hippies were living. That's where I met Beverly D'Angelo and Robert Blake.

She said her name was Wendy, and she lived in Bel Air, where she collected hook rugs. She had a pile of them that needed fixing.

I went to her house to pick a few up. I looked at her collection, and she had quite a few that needed fixing.

"Don't take them all; I want to see if I like how you do it."

She asked me to bring them over to Sony Studios in Culver City for her. She sent someone down to the gate to pick them up. When she called me, she said, "They came out great. Please pick up some more."

I fixed them all. I kept calling but couldn't get her, so I just put them away for a while, and waited.

I forgot about it, which sometimes happens in my business, and I left them on the side, waiting to be picked up. When the Academy Awards came up, *Forrest Gump* won for best picture.

Who marched up the stairs to collect the award, but Wendy Finerman, from Sony Pictures!?

Later in the week I called to congratulate her, and told her I'd forgotten about the rugs. She had, too, and told me to bring them to the house. She loved them, and introduced me to her then-husband, the producer, Mark Canton. I went into the living room, and there it was, the Academy Award. "Go pick it up," she said. I did.

Years later, when I finished my screenplay, *The Botany Club*, I sent it to Wendy Finerman Productions, and she was kind enough to respond, although she opted instead to do *The Devil Wears Prada*.

When I was a kid in high school, there was an article in *Life* Magazine on the ten biggest and best high school players in the country. My high school had one: Billy Hathaway. Also mentioned in the article was a guy from Philadelphia named Wilt "the Stilt" Chamberlain. I followed his career from Kansas to the NBA, and I read that he could also high-jump, shot-put, and throw the discus. I realized that he could have been the greatest decathlon champion who ever lived, and I remembered seeing him briefly in a few clubs in New York, dancing. It looked like he was standing on a table, and everybody else was in a hole. Of course, I read all those articles about him sleeping with ten thousand women.

One afternoon on Coldwater, he pulled up and got out of a car. He just kept getting out, getting bigger and bigger... There he was, seven foot three. We talked about rugs, we talked about basketball, we talked about Larry Brown, my buddy from high school, the ex-coach at Kansas who finally won a pro championship. We talked about the clubs, and he started talking about a few of his women. He had just finished a volleyball game down at the beach. I had a large selection of pillows for sale, and he was lying on them. We had spent a few hours together, when he pulled out a few hundred dollar bills, picked up a few pillows, and said, "I love your office. Keep it up, kid."

Robert Blake got out of a black car, his hair dyed black, wearing black boots, black pants, a black shirt, and black sunglasses. He was truly the Man in Black.

I was trying to connect with him, but our radios were on two different frequencies: I was on FM and he was on AM. I told him where the rugs came from and how they were made and their history, and he repeated it to me just as I had told him. This went on for about a half-hour. I don't remember if he bought anything or if he just left. Very strange.

Finally, as the season turned, the police found me. The charge: peddling on private property. I had a peddler's license, but I hadn't realized it would be a problem since I had Kirsch's permission.

Two policemen got out of a car. They had their hands on their weapons; it felt like *Dragnet*. I showed them I had a permit, license, and registration, all the proper forms. "Just the facts, sir, just the facts."

They gave me a big citation and told me the judge was looking forward to talking to me about my adventures. They added that a lot of people had gotten into a lot of trouble, and they were pulling people off the roads. The bonsai guy didn't look happy, either.

My day in court arrived. I decided I had to put on a disguise. I wanted to make sure I wasn't going to get a stiff fine, and I also didn't want to be recognized. Obviously, if I came in with an Armani suit and a pinky ring I'd be in for thousands, but it also wouldn't do for any clients to recognize me. And, I admit, I was looking for sympathy from the judge. I wanted to blend in—and be invisible. So I parted my hair in the middle, buttoned my shirt from the 1920s which I'd found at the Salvation Army with matching pants, oversize shoes, huge glasses, and a stained tie, and I covered some of my teeth with black paper so I'd look like I was missing a few.

I drove down to court and entered the large room. The place was packed. I had to sit between two people. They were both eating, even though the sign said *No Eating, No Smoking*.

The hours went by; I had my *Wall Street Journal* hidden in an old *Life* Magazine. They kept giving people fines. Some people had already been there ten times, and the judge knew them personally. It was old school: ten days! Two weeks! Probation! Five hundred dollar fine! Eight hundred dollar fine!

They called my name, and I waddled down to the bench. The judge looked at me, lifted his glasses up. "First offense?"

"Yes, sir!"

"A hundred dollars! I never want to see you again!"

The bail bondsman gave me back my papers, and he wrinkled his nose as if to say, "Don't get too close to me."

That was my last selling day on the side of the road. They told me that if they caught me again they would take all my stuff and lock me up for a while. Never again, I vowed.

Chapter 20:
Trials and Tribulations

There used to be "Creekers"—they lived along Topanga Creek.

In the 1950s people came to Topanga to fish and hike, and it was their second home. Many people in the arts and music world would come there, in the '60s and '70s, like Will Geer, Arlo Guthrie, Charles Manson, Julie Christie, and Warren Beattie, who ran in and out of Weenie's restaurant.

There used to be old pickup trucks, '60s cars, bib overalls, and hillbillies. Now there are Range Rovers, Hummers, Beamers, Mercedes, and Volkswagens. There are the latte ladies and the kids on computers.

I used to sit on the porch in front of my shop, and Anthony Hopkins would pull up in his old Ford, sit down, visit with me, pick out some beautiful rugs, and ask if it was okay if he gave me a check.

Now we have *Sideways*—people slide in, try to buy something, chisel, re-chisel, run down with a drop of cash, leap in their cars, and never come back.

One afternoon it was about ninety degrees in Topanga. This cute little girl came bouncing out of a car with a nice Texas accent and said somebody recommended her. I didn't have my rolling boys over to roll rugs. I said to her, "Why don't you come back and we can take pictures?"

"No big deal, let's unroll 'em, you and me."

We spent the next two hours rolling around the floor opening up heavy rugs, dripping with sweat, and sharing ice teas. Finally, she picked up three or four rugs.

"Could I send a bill to my managers' office and they'll cut you a check?" She'd just finished working on a movie with Tom Cruise. It was called *Jerry Maguire*, and she was Renée Zellweger.

I didn't know who she was. My wife told me she was a star, but what a nice person, so unassuming and gracious. Thank you, Renée. I needed the money at the time.

I went up in my blue truck with my day worker, Lorenzo, who looked like a Mayan Indian, with his jet black hair and square shoulders, and we started hanging rugs out in the kiosk.

Adjacent to the kiosk and Topanga Home Grown was a fifty-foot railroad tie, and behind that was Moon's Market, which had old food sold as fresh food, vegetables in dated cans at a discount, and a "hot appetizer counter" where they sold sandwiches. They also sold wine, beer, and everything you could buy from a large supermarket that was open seven days a week.

This drew the locals, to buy their food and provisions, even at inflated prices. I didn't mind that so much, but the people who sat on that railroad tie were another matter. These were the Creekers. Some were homeless, some were indigenous day workers, and some were old and young "tweakers" (meth users). They were either drunk, fighting with each other or being loud and boisterous and rude. And I was right next to them, trying to sell rugs from five hundred dollars to four thousand.

I tried to talk to them—they saw me as a stranger, and I got no cooperation.

On the other side were the locals who came down to talk to Steve Carlson at his restaurant, the Willows, and have a drink after work. They were impossible. They were drug addicts, alcoholics, and construction workers. Don't get me wrong, they weren't bad people, and I did fish with them occasionally, but they were oblivious to my trying to earn a living.

Several locals came by and explained to me very nicely that I was wasting my time trying to sell anything in Topanga Canyon because the people were too cheap. But I knew that twenty thousand cars a day went through that canyon, and some of their drivers lived in the affluent areas of the Valley—or Calabasas, or Tarzana. They had money, and I always believed that quality would sell itself. Within thirty days, we were making money on that corner.

Steve Carlson and his wife, Leslie, owned the property that is now Pine Tree Circle. Interestingly enough, they bought it from my old buddy in crime, Weenie. They were kind enough to offer me half of the trailer to put my rugs in, so I could bring more inventory and hang the rugs all around the trailer. That worked well. People pulled into the parking lot, and the money kept coming in.

I was also getting recommendations as people spread the word from Coldwater and Laurel Canyon to Malibu at Broad Beach in Trancas, and these folks started calling me.

Steven and Leslie offered me a shop across the street on the corner. I jumped at the chance, and took the entire trailer across the street and put it behind this shop. I started building onto it and making it grow: bedroom, kitchen, office—it became Topanga Rugs, a minor institution. On the weekends in the summer, we opened at ten, and I worked until it got dark. I put lights around it, and those were the good times.

It was a beautiful environment, even though it was along the road. I had a big oak tree and lots of porch furniture, and for the first few years, my dogs, Huey and Ginger, would greet the customers. All my friends and acquaintances would come by and introduce their friends. It was a happening.

Steve and Leslie were from Long Island, where I hailed from as well, so we had a lot in common. We got together with a group of guys from Willows, their new restaurant, and started chartering boats down in San Diego for one- and two-day trips for albacore, yellowtail, and dorado. We'd all drive down the night before, go to a Chinese restaurant, drink and eat, pass out on the boat and then motor one hundred and twenty miles down off Ensenada, and fish. It was like being out with a bunch of pirates. I never was a big drinker, fortunately. They could outdrink most people that I ever knew, but most of them would get up the next morning at six and start to fish.

These trips became rituals, and everybody looked forward to

them. We always added a few new faces, and we always caught fish. We had the right boat, and the right luck.

Everything was going smoothly. We were able to go on some nice trips, buy beautiful merchandise, and meet interesting people, until George W. Bush got elected President.

Having lived in Dallas, I'd heard rumors about how George W. ran the Texas Rangers and would fall asleep in meetings, and how Daddy and some of his buddies bought W. the team to give him something to do. Never in my wildest nightmares did I ever think this fratboy and practicing alcoholic would become President of the United States.

I remember hearing stories about Wild George: drunken nights in Dallas or at the football games. And from the first days he got elected and started with his great tax cuts, my business started to go down—and gas started to go up. And then 9-11 happened, and all his buddies from Saudi Arabia, with whom he still holds hands, left, and our economy started to spiral.

Soon thereafter, construction began next to me on Pine Tree Circle, a two-story shopping center. The banging, the digging, the rains, the rocks falling in the road, the washing-out of the roads, the earthquakes, the floods, the unbearable heat in the summer... but we got through it to the other side.

•◊•◊•

I had a lot of time to pass, and read everything I could get my hands on. Two, three, four books a week—from light paperbacks to serious books, as books had become a great passion for me.

I once asked a friend of mine, "How do you become a writer?" And he said, "Read, read, and then read some more. And watch and listen, and then read some more." And so I did, and then some. But it was time to put it down on paper.

One night, I got a jolt—and it wasn't an earthquake. A voice said, "Get a paper and pencil." I didn't feel like getting up to get a paper and pencil in the middle of the night, and just thought I'd had a bad dream. I tried to go back to sleep, but a voice in my head kept urging me to write.

So I started to take notes and scribble things down and did an outline. I sent my wife to Santa Monica College to learn about screenwriting, since I didn't have the time or the patience, and the last writing I had done had been in 1962 at Emerson College in a literature class. Plus, being dyslexic, the words come out backwards.

Diana went to school, and when they told her she had to write an outline for a screenplay, I gave her the outline to my piece. The teacher gave it an A+, and she started to work on it. We got about thirty pages into it, and then the Northridge earthquake hit. It was the middle of the night, my cat flew up in the air, my dog lurched sideways, and it sounded like a freight train went through my living room as everything went upside down. That was the end of that project for a while.

•◊•◊•

A friend of Diana's became a personal assistant to an actor who plays action heroes. We'll call him Stanley Stunning.

I received a call that Mr. Stunning was going to Morocco to make a movie, and he wanted to know about buying rugs. I gave the PA a lengthy explanation, told her the cities where he could get the best prices, the stores in Casablanca, what to look for, and I offered guidelines on how much to pay.

I enjoyed Mr. Stunning's acting work, and thought helping him might help me to get some business and recommendations.

About a year later, I got a call from someone else who said she was Mr. and Mrs. Stunning's personal assistant. Mr. Stunning had just bought a bunch of rugs in Morocco as I'd suggested, probably for his new house in Malibu, and he wasn't happy with them.

I said, "Let me see if I can help you."

I met the assistant at a warehouse in Santa Monica. It was loaded with their Moroccan rugs, several very nice Orientals, and some beautiful Aubusson decorative tapestries. I offered to sell them for Mr. and Mrs. Stunning.

I picked up all of the Moroccan rugs and put them in my shop. There must have been a half a dozen, and they were big. I sold a few of them and forwarded the money to the assistant.

She then asked me to try to sell the Orientals and see what I could do with the tapestries. I was able to sell the Orientals at the prices I'd told them I could get, and sent them more funds. I took the two beautiful tapestries and brought them to New York.

Everybody wanted to buy them cheaply. Finally, I was able to sell them in L.A. I wasn't completely through with the deal, but they were out of my hands and I was waiting to get the money cleared.

I received a phone call from the personal assistant telling me that they wanted the tapestries back. I explained that I'd already contracted to sell them, and the deal was pending.

Evidently, the people who originally sold the tapestries to the Stunnings at an inflated price heard about them being back on the market and called them and said that they could get twice or three times as much as I was getting for them.

Unfortunately, my deal had been completed by that time, and I was ready to submit the funds.

And all hell broke loose.

I received a barrage of phone calls from lawyers telling me that I'd stolen the tapestries and converted them illegally. I let the callers know that I'd been working for the Stunnings for two years, and had been giving them money for their rugs all along, as we'd agreed. What were they talking about? They continued to harass me for weeks, until finally a detective from the L.A. police department called and said that the Stunnings wanted to put a warrant out for my arrest, for theft. The cop was sympathetic and understood where I was coming from, but the harassing calls kept coming.

We settled the matter; they got the tapestries back, and they got their money.

•◇•◇•

I was told by the Carlsons that the County might acquire the land behind my shop and build a library for Topanga. They felt that it probably wouldn't happen, but they were letting me know that if it did happen, the library entrance would be right where my gallery was.

It happened.

I had very mixed reactions. I was saddened, because this meant I would surely be leaving Topanga. The spot was right across the street from old Topanga, and had its charm, as well as the best visibility and location. But I did feel that I had been waiting to get out of there, and clearly this was my sign. The

County said they would compensate me for the condemnation.

Meanwhile, I was sending rugs to several locations in San Miguel de Allende, in Mexico. And they were selling them there. So there was money to have a good life down there. And I had the product that they liked, needed, and appreciated. These people had the sensibility one needs to appreciate and acquire these kinds of rugs and tapestries.

We kept hearing that they were having meetings about the Topanga library. And people would come and measure things. Finally, the story broke in the Topanga paper, with a rendering of a fifteen million-dollar library right behind us.

Slowly we consolidated the shop and put up signs: *Going out of Business Sale*. Before that I had put up signs that said *Staying in Business Sale*. I think the majority of the people in Topanga who saw the signs didn't actually think we were going to leave, even though it was in the papers, and the people driving by probably thought it was just another "going out of business" gimmick.

But it worked. People showed up and bought things. And that kept us going. Still, it was time to say goodbye and head south.

As the real estate boomed, the old Topangans who had bought houses for twenty thousand dollars saw their houses go up to a million; and they smartly took the money. They were teachers, social workers, painters, artists—regular people who raised families in Topanga.

Replacing them were dot-com magnates, screenwriters, movie stars, lawyers, plastic surgeons, some Europeans and Australians who had previously lived in Venice, Los Feliz and West Hollywood. They were younger, driven, and ruthless. It was Generation X and the *Me* Generation. They didn't particularly care what they were buying, where it was made, or its history— they just wanted it to work with their shabby chic couch. All they wanted to do was throw me their credit card, throw their rugs in the car and go pick up their kids from school or go have a latte. I was no longer dealing with fine art—it was fashion and commerce.

Some of them would bring the rugs back after a month; they were bored, they wanted new ones. They didn't mind paying more money. They traded up or down, as their consciousness changed.

Then there was the group that had dogs and other pets that would damage the rugs. They would bring them in for cleaning, and they were always wet and smelly. There were women who came in every month to have the same rug cleaned. And then, at the end, they would ask why the rug was falling apart? It was my fault.

It was commerce and very difficult for me. We'd go to the store, clear the energy, work, and people would occasionally interrupt us to ask for directions or buy something. But this was not Masar-i Sharif with the old souls moving around. There were 30,000 cars a day on that road, chasing away most of the good energy.

We had a little room in the back, which I built to look like a fishing boat with two bunk beds, and when traffic was too heavy, or I needed to stay overnight, I slept there. In dreamtime, Indians and animals came. The spot gave me a spinning sensation, similar to the one I've felt in Sedona, Santa Fe, and Masar-i Sharif, and it seemed to be very strong in my one hundred square feet. Others who stayed there, either for a nap or overnight, felt the same thing, and some reported healings.

My first inkling that I'd soon be leaving the area came with the Malibu fires. It was early afternoon, the fire engines were screaming down the road, and people were running down toward the shop with their horses and dogs, heading toward the beach. I waited an extra hour, but the fires kept moving steadily closer, so I loaded up my truck with my best valuables and headed down to the beach.

As I drove, every time I looked in the rear-view mirror, all I could see was fire. The van grew hotter and hotter. It felt like *The Ten Commandments*. By the time I made the last left turn and reached the beach, the sky was red and the hills were on fire. It took hours to navigate through all the chaos and get home.

By the time the county finally bought the property from me, I was more than ready to leave. I was tired of handling urine-stained wool for a bunch of spoiled rich people, even though I had been well compensated. It was bittersweet, but ultimately I didn't mind leaving.

Goodbye, Creekers, keep on creekin'. I'm outta here.

Chapter 21:

San Miguel de Allende, the Crystal City

2 008: A man walked into the International Hotel in Kabul, fully armed with grenades and other weapons, into the ladies' spa. He shot them and called them infidels. He ran up and down the hallways shooting at others, jumped on someone, and blew himself up. A sign of the times.

It took weeks to pack all our stuff in Santa Monica. I was loading my big Volvo wagon—daily, it seemed—with all sorts of herbs, books, and good paintings. Before we left, we went to a New Year's Eve party at the Playboy mansion—our twentieth party there, together. When the bus pulled up we saw that it was still decorated for Christmas; quite a sight. Inside, the place was already gyrating. Eye candy, some screaming queens, body-painted dancers, an endless array of gourmet delights, and libations, celebrities galore—all the beautiful people strutting their stuff—everyone dressed to the nines.

And then there was the grotto, the fondling—the usual fare. But this one was the best of Hef; a perfect way to say goodbye.

One morning at nine-thirty, we slid down the street, stopped by Santa Monica Homeopathic, picked up our herbs and headed for the ten to San Miguel de Allende, Mexico. We pulled off in Palm Springs for a bite to eat, then moved on to Tucson. Bumper to bumper traffic. This I wouldn't miss. We stopped at a Best Western for the night, and then we were back on the road.

We had to get off that road onto a secondary one. After a mad toad ride, we were confronted with hill after hill, huge buses, and a two-lane highway with two lanes of trucks spewing diesel fuel in our faces.

On and on, battling potholes, monster trucks, belching cars, bad directions, winding roads, rutted roads, donkeys, horses, cows, night specters, the fear of being stopped by the police or, worse, being kidnapped. We got lost and more lost in this surreal nightmare. Till, at certain times, when it seemed impossibly difficult, angels interceded in the guise of local people—to help us, to save us. And throughout, we were actually bestowed some grace, some fun, some enchanting moments.

Finally, we arrived, dust-bitten and exhausted. Two days later the car wouldn't start. It had died. I had broken its heart; it had had enough of me.

•◊•◊•

I called San Miguel de Allende "the Crystal City" because crystals and quartz were everywhere; it was a mining town where the stones were dug up and used for building.

It was like Topanga used to be. People said hello to each other. *¡Buenos dias! ¡Buenas tardes! ¡Buenas noches!* Everybody answered with a smile—no attitudes. The light was soft, as it used to be in Topanga, before all the traffic. And the stars at night were heavenly there—as they still are in Topanga. Horses trod down the cobblestone streets, and donkeys were tied up in front of people's houses. There were lots of creeks, gullies, and canals that filled up during the rain. And you could hear the insects at night—the crickets and bugs—and birds abounded.

As for the highly-educated and arts-oriented expatriate community of San Miguel, there were artisans, designers, and architects, the big, rich Texans and the weird, educated people from Berkeley, Harvard, Cambridge, and Oxford of the sixties, and the Sorbonne, as well as intellectuals and professionals from

South America. There were also packs of old predatory wolves—looking for somebody's platinum American Express Card.

Around the perimeter were old mines. There was a silver prospecting area adjacent to San Miguel. When the mines were dug, they took some of the quartz from the surface and brought it into the city, and built out. Also, around the circumference of San Miguel were hot springs with mineral waters. It was almost as if a volcano erupted around the edge of the city and never quite settled—it still bubbled with heat and water.

These rocks and crystals were used for the sidewalks and the streets. You could imagine how each rock was different—nothing was uniform; you needed a good pair of shoes to maneuver around the city. One daydreaming moment your ankle buckled, and you were down. It was difficult, because the architecture was so beautiful, and the people were so interesting, that you couldn't keep from looking around. And the sky was so blue that it was hard to focus down. I think I finally figured it out after stumbling a few times and twisting a few ankles: one eye up and one eye down. It was an art.

There was one curb I measured that was literally thirty-eight inches high. You needed a running start to get up on that one. And along the edge of the curb's cobblestones were little irrigation ditches. If you weren't careful, you could step in and lose your shoe.

There were many senior citizens. I heard of people going to the hospital with hips, legs, and arms broken, and I saw many people with arm slings and abrasions on their forehead.

But they were good sports, and they kept coming back, nonetheless.

On most of the streets it wasn't possible to walk side by side with somebody. Or, if you walked your dog, it had to be in front of you. It was like Europe: lots of motorcycles, little tiny cars, donkeys, and lots of chickens.

So you really had to be one leg up and down on the other one. Men on the outside, women on the inside. If you made the mistake (a woman on the outside), you got the *Look*; I hated the *Look*.

These things were very important if you were to survive in San Miguel.

On the weekends, starting about 6 a.m., there was always a festival. The festival for the dead, the festival for the living, the festival for the saints, a festival for the revolution, the Constitution, the prostitution! They had a hundred festivals a year. There were frequent parades and music in the streets. They had a custom which I couldn't quite understand: frequent fireworks. They'd set fireworks off at four or five in the morning during the festivals. I grew accustomed to it, but in the beginning it felt like I was in Iraq or Afghanistan in a firefight. You did get used to the noise, but, at first, it was troubling. Best to bring earplugs.

The people were a mix from Sedona, San Miguel, 1920s Paris, and Greenwich Village. You would also see cowboy hats, tight jeans and boots, and large Rolexes.

It was a good mix, and everybody seemed to get along. Very seldom—almost never—did I hear a raised voice. A cab driver might scream when he ran into a pole by accident, or somebody dropped a bunch of tamales off their head—say, women when they were carrying them down the street—but I never heard any arguments about money, or attitudes.

The *gringos* respected the locals, and the locals knew the money that the *gringos* were spending kept the economy going. Everybody appeared to have a job, except for the older generation sitting in the parks, the restaurants, the art schools, and the library, waiting for their social security checks and annuities.

It appeared to me that there were too many American women with dyed hair, plastic surgery, gargantuan lips, lipo, lots of jewelry, and ethnic outfits, looking for love in all the wrong places. I'd hear them in the bars and the restaurants, in the packs, running with the dogs, looking for Stanley Stunning. They were looking for Mr. Perfect to use his platinum card, his IRA, and be taken care of.

They'd ask me questions, as if I were back in a bar in the '70s. What was my sign? Where was I from?

The expatriate guys in San Miguel were burnt out from three marriages and paying alimony, spending the money to fix their teeth, besides their own plastic surgeries. They'd supported enough women and children for many lifetimes and just wanted to be left alone to drink, and put their face in the sun.

And *if* they wanted somebody to spend a few years with or a few nights with, they would want someone fresh and young and tight, who would draw over them the blanket of illusion, and make them feel young again—not some wrinkled lizard, her eyes clouded over by her own fears of aging.

But then again, I'm jaded and perverse.

The ratio of available women to men in San Miguel was 10-to-1. And the *1* sometimes had a walker! So the women needed to beware—and put on their best face.

•◇•◇•

I stumbled into an AA meeting in San Antonio, off Rancho San Antonio. There too the ratio was 10 to 1. The meeting was run by three lesbian arm-wrestlers. Short hair, chunky, and demanding. I've been to quite a few meetings over the years—Alanons, AAs, and so forth. I don't have the disease, but I drop in every once in a while to hear the things that I need to hear.

These women were aggressive. They took charge, and dictated policy, and did not follow Bill Wilson's Big Book. They were judgmental and tough.

After an hour, I couldn't wait to get the hell out of there.

I walked down the street along San Antonio—it was about 90 degrees—past the Allende Institute. Fumes poured out of cars, students carried books, and old ladies had their hands out for a *peso* to buy a meal.

I saw a beautiful Labrador begging by the door of a bookstore, and I kept walking. Then I saw an ancient man pushing a cart with colored shaved ices up a hill. It was a pretty steep hill to go up, even without anything to push. He was all gnarly, had a cracked straw hat, and wore a heavy shirt, *harachis* with leather soles, and the white pants that the country people wear.

He was huffing and puffing to get up the hill, and cars and trucks were honking at him because he was in the way.

I walked out in the street and grabbed the cart for him, and started pushing. He looked at me and grabbed my hand, but I pushed the cart up the hill for about fifteen minutes. It was heavy.

I tried speaking to him in broken Spanish, saying, "Much work you do! You make much money?"

"I live out in the country. I've been doing this for 60 years." He said he was born close to 1907 and was almost a hundred years old.

We both pushed the cart up the hill, and people looked at me as if I was a weirdo. I noticed people leaning out of buses and pointing.

When we were almost at the top of the hill, he pointed to the left, and I helped him push the cart over to a spot in front of a local grocery store.

He grabbed my hand, gave me a hug, and looked in my eyes. His were deep brown. I can't help thinking of The Old Man and the Sea, and, for a flash of a second, I thought I saw my father's eyes.

As I left him and started walking down the street, some people looked at me quietly.

Since then, I haven't seen him. Nobody knows where he is. He passed me some energy when he held my hand and looked into my soul, some *shaktipat,* I feel sure of it.

Maybe he retired. I'll keep looking for him.

•◊•◊•

I was walking Emmanuel, my rescued dog, near Juarez Park one Saturday when I saw another purebred Lab looking at me. Just staring.

It was a big dog, and, for some reason, I was a bit concerned about this one being off leash. He quietly came over to my dog, and Emmanuel got a little tense. Then he started licking my hands.

A Mexican guy walked by, and I asked him if it was his dog. "No."

The Lab followed me into the lot. I let Emmanuel off the leash and the two dogs ran around, chasing each other, for fifteen minutes.

When it was time to return home, the Lab followed us back. He walked right into the house with me, and I noticed how skinny he was. He wasn't dirty, he was perfectly groomed, he had clean ears and nails, and he could sit and obey commands in English, but he was emaciated.

We posted him on the Civil List where people put notices.

Nothing happened. The dog spent Saturday night at our place, and I put him outside on our roof deck, and noticed that he was drinking a lot of water and eating a lot of food.

The next day, I put him on a leash and took him over to a neighbor who knows everything about the neighborhood.

"Have you ever seen this dog?"

"No. He looks like an indoor dog, doesn't he?"

Walking back home, we ran into three dogs—a big Dalmatian, and two other ratty-looking dogs. They attacked the Lab. I kicked the Dalmatian in the ribs and the other two got away. The Lab had put his tail between his legs and did nothing to defend himself.

I took the dog into the house and put it up on the roof for the night.

The next day I let him in, and later I took him and Emmanuel to the park. I was getting very fond of this dog, but I didn't know what to do with him. I was feeding him, though, and we were bonding.

The next morning, I went into town to do some errands. While at the *Jardín*, I asked various people if they know the dog.

Suddenly, a very well-dressed Mexican woman shouted, "That's my dog! That's Coco!"

And the Lab yelped and leapt into her arms. They were both crying, and two of the woman's friends were also crying— a reunion.

I had dressed the dog up with a bandanna, and given it a name and an identity.

I finally said, "I know this is your dog, but it looks very skinny—don't you feed it?"

She said the dog had just gotten away that Saturday, and had been diagnosed with a malignant growth, and been given chemotherapy. He might be dying.

She took the dog back, and I gave her my card.

The dog looked over his shoulder at me and smiled a thank you, the way Labradors can.

The bell rang and she brought me a big box of cookies and the leash.

"I just wanted to thank you. My kids were praying on their knees to the saints, and they knew he was still alive."

•◊•◊•

Sitting in a restaurant with Diana and some friends, I saw posters on the wall identical to the ones outside the ring of the ten *corridas* that summer when Weenie and I were in Spain—a lifetime ago. The posters came alive. I could see the *torero* with his scarlet cape as the bull ran full speed, his horns flashing in the sun. I could hear the crowd and feel the movement of the tightly woven bodies moving back and forth in rhythm with this dance to the death. In my reminiscing, I began to tell them the story in between bites of fajitas.

The year was 1963. It was one hundred two degrees in the great bullring in Madrid. The guys and I were sitting there with girls we picked up, drinking wine and hallucinogens out of a goatskin. I was waiting for Tyrone Power to come out, as in *Blood in the Sand*, and do his number. I didn't know what I was doing there, because I liked animals. When I saw the picadors weakening the bull, I got nauseated and wanted to leave. But I stayed. I didn't want to be a pussy. Hemingway sat there, the macho man, so why couldn't I?

The bull came out and lumbered across the ring. I felt I was right there with the bullfighter. It wasn't a high school football game, or a wrestling match, or a track meet, or pole vaulting through the air, but I definitely had a surge of adrenaline and could identify with the *torero*. The bull rushed forward as the *torero* turned his back to it, and the crowd screamed, *"¡Ole!"* They sized each other up as the bull made three or four passes at the bullfighter. It was very hot, and I was sitting in the cheap seats in the sun.

Finally, the bull seemed to get the upper hand and caught the *torero*'s thigh with his horn. The crowd *oohed* and held their breath. He was off-balance. Amazingly, he got down on his knee, held the cape in front of the bull, and stared him in the eyes. They both froze, as I did. Then he took control. Left, right, left, right—passes (*pases naturales*) and graceful veronicas. The animal was bleeding, and you could see he was weakening.

It was time for the kill. The *torero* got up on his toes, bringing the bull's head down lower and lower with passes, and then he lunged, plunging the sword between the head and the shoulders.

The bull staggered, shook, and went down. The crowd roared with approval, and it was time for rewards. He cut both ears and the tail off. People threw flowers at him as the sun started to set. It grew cooler. The sand was wet with blood.

Every day in San Miguel was an adventure. A door opened, and you peeked in. The maid was cleaning or somebody was getting something delivered. It looked like an old, weather-beaten door, but behind this door were magnificent gardens, antique urns, wrought-iron masterpieces, and rooms that went on, and on, and on. Each one was different; every door was different.

The dogs barked at night. They were left to guard empty houses while their people were in Mexico City or Guadalahara and came back for the weekend. Guadayana, where I lived, used to be full of old orchards. There were still some empty lots, like the ones I used to play in as a young boy. In the evenings, every hour on the hour, I heard a policeman on horseback come by, patrolling the neighborhood. I was on a little hill, and if I walked up fifty feet, there was a 16th century church that served the local neighborhood. No gringos went there. Across from that was a little *tienda* where you could get a Coca-Cola, beans, rice or a sweet treat. They were all owned by Ma and Pa, and the television was always on in the background, on some soap opera.

Dogs were barking, children were laughing in the streets, I smelled the tortillas being baked, and there was thunder echoing through the sky.

From my roof, I had a panoramic view of the city, the mountains, and the churches. I'd sit on my hammock, reading, with my dog, Emmanuel, at my feet. Mr. Red-Eyes was gone, and I was at peace as the sun set—the mountains disappearing in the distance.

Epilogue

I liked the fact that you didn't need a car in San Miguel. Everything was done on foot. You were forced to go to the gym every day. The inclines were wonderful. They'd burn your buns as well as your quads. It was very painful. But it was worth it.

You could go anywhere you wanted on a bus for 40 cents, and they had little green cabs for two dollars that would take you around the city.

Costumes were good: strong work boots, pants with lots of pockets, a knapsack, a backpack, water, a good hat, sunscreen, and off you went.

The average temperature was 71 degrees. They did have their rainy season in the summer, in the afternoons. The water flowed down into the streets from the mountains, and, if you weren't careful, it could knock you off your feet. Two hours later, the water was gone and it was dry. April started the rains, and May was warm. Between two and five each afternoon you were looking for that siesta.

The nights could get quite chilly. And usually by ten thirty, except on the weekends, the streets were empty. There was no crime; I had no paranoia.

After you were finished with a meal, nobody would dare ever bring you a check. You had to ask for it.

They were happy to serve you, they bowed and bent and were polite. They didn't throw your food at you like the would-be actors who work in the restaurants in L.A. They had a union for the waiters. It was a very good job to have. Sure beat digging a ditch or building a pyramid.

You woke up in the morning, you could hear the birds. But before the birds, you heard the dogs. It usually started around five, when they'd talk to each other.

And there were dogs to the left and dogs to the right, dogs everywhere... Some belonged to people behind huge estates where they had two, three, four dogs in a house, and some dogs lived in packs in the streets. They weren't aggressive. The dogs on the streets all had their tails between their legs, and were shivering with cold. This was one of the unfortunate things.

I'd never been in a place where so many people cared more about their dogs than about other people. But everybody had a dog. Everybody cared. I guess it was a form of displaced compensation for people who didn't have wives, husbands, or children—they had dogs, cats, birds, iguanas... They'd take care of them, they'd nurture them, and they'd talk about them over dinner, over lunch, and over breakfast.

I got up, and walked down my street. As I opened the door, I saw beautiful bougainvillea blooming and kids walking in green uniforms to church. I made a left turn and walked down my street towards Juarez Park. It looked like a Pendergrass painting. Kids with balloons, little booths selling food, and a basketball court with French floral designs. It was a real European garden.

I walked through there, smelling the flowers. That month they were having *Candelária*. They brought flowers in from all over the countryside and sold them for a month. Day and night, they lived in their trucks, and the families all stayed together. It was wonderful to see. We tried to help them.

Everywhere I went, people were saying *"Buenos días, señor,"* and I responded in kind. It was wonderful to have everyone say good morning and smile. Nobody looked down at their feet unless it was to avoid falling in a hole. People looked you in the eye, it was great.

The men had straw hats and the Indian women were carrying their children. The kids were actually singing on their way to school. I found myself behind them as they sang in sequence. It was enchanting.

Going into town, I passed by all the beautiful little bed-and-breakfasts and the little shops. You could smell the coffee brewing and the pastries heating. On the street corner you could get a large fruit drink or a vegetable drink for a dollar. And if you were hungry, there were wonderful chicken tacos and beef tacos with all the trimmings—and a smile.

I went into the main *jardín* and sat down. You could buy the *New York Times* from Julio, who sold them on the corner. Sitting on the bench with your cappuccino or your fruit drink, you could look directly at the *Parroquia*, one of the ten greatest churches in the world. It was pink and gray and taupe, it was fabulous.

From there, my decision was whether to go to the baths and get a massage or go up to the Tuesday market, which was about ten acres of shops, food, groceries, and vendors. It looked like the Rose Bowl but with food.

I looked up at the lapis blue sky, with a tinge of French blue and puffy clouds. I closed my eyes and felt the vibration of the earth. I'd been told that I'd been here in other incarnations. It felt safe, warm, as if hands were wrapped around me, protecting me. I was home at last. I didn't know what was going to be coming in the future, but I was sure I was in a safe spot. I was sitting on the crystal. It was under my feet.

I saw years flashing by, different centuries, different sounds. I went up, up, my arms were straight back, my hair was blowing in the wind.

I was going down a tunnel, and I was home.

So it was.

Gallery

This is my father's mother's family in Kiev, in the Ukraine. They were merchants.
I never heard much about that side of the family.

1958. We just soundly beat Oceanside High School on the gridiron (with Ed Evans).
Jeez – was I ever really that young?

1964. Fort Dix, New Jersey. Learning the spirit of the bayonet: Kill! I paid the guy an extra dollar to go easy on me and not take it all off. Look at what happened.

REAGAN WILSON
MISS OCTOBER 1967

1967. Playboy publicity shot of Diana, whose professional name is Reagan Wilson.

1970. Some of my clients going in to watch the Ali–Bonavena fight on December 7.

1970. Funky auto, NYC, outside MSG for Ali-Bonavena fight.

1970. Some of my other acquaintances on their way to the fight.

1972. Philip and me on a shark-hunt off Montauk (LI, NY).

1977. Modeling photo of Diana in her apartment on
Riverside Drive in New York City. This is what she was wearing
the night I met her.

1978. 2AM, just awoke, need to get over to Studio 54 for a business meeting.

In downtown Kabul, Afghanistan – I had just made a new friend.

1980. In Santa Barbara with my dad, at a scenic point.
The Pacific was so clear and so blue.

1981. In Dallas, on the phone, probably haggling with a customer.

1983. Pondering what to do next
(Savannah, Ga – still up from night before).

1983. Santa Fe, NM – on the way to the Baroness Taj's dinner party,
wearing new shades.

DALLAS YMCA TURKEY TROT
November 26, 1987
SPORT PHOTO

1987. Gobbling – I mean hobbling along –
at the Dallas YMCA Turkey Trot.

1995. A shot for Buzz Magazine LA. Behind us – rugs, of course.

1998. In front of my new gallery in Topanga Canyon (Ca).

1999. New Year's Eve. Hef with his three roomies, before his nuptials.

1999. They think I'm wishing everyone a Happy New Year, but I'm really just making noise.

2001-2002. Married and still in love after several decades.
At Hef's place on New Year's Eve to ring in the New Year.

2005. In Topanga Canyon (Ca) with Ed Evans and Eddie Lauter. Evans(L): ABC sports cameraman. Lauter (R): famous character actor. The connection?
Long Beach High School (Long Island, NY).

2005. R&R in lovely
San Miguel de Allende
(Mexico).

Diana with Tom Hanks at a gala for the Apollo project.
Can you tell he was still filming Castaway?

2005. Helen Antonaccio, me and Reagan (Diana) at a
Midsummer Night's Dream party.

2007. Reagan, Hef, Nancy Harwood and Kimberly Hefner on New Year's Eve.

2010. Revisiting the scene of the crime on a trip back to NY.

2010. Reagan and her best friend, fellow Playmate Nancy Harwood – biker chicks.

2014. Recent headshot of Diana by Barry Denton at his ranch in Prescott, Arizona.

Acknowledgments

MY THANKS TO:

Brilliant Michael Claibourne, who never gave up.

Philip Carlo, for watching my back.

L. Mark Newman, for not drowning.

Steady Eddie Evans, for being steady.

Anthony J. Michaels, for being there.

Maddie Patty, for the spirit she is.

Fast Black, for helping me escape.

Zach Leary, for all the insight on his father.

Contessa Christina Paolozzi, for keeping me on my game.

Hef, for all the free meals and all the great company.

Steve and Leslie Carlson, my Topanga family.

Bill Pearlman, who put his 1960's eyes on the manuscript.

Andrea Pennington, MD, who offered empowerment and healing.

Bernie and Betty Hoeg, my Missoula family, for their patience and insight.

Steven Joseph, who said it was good enough to do, and then gave it a very coherent edit.

David Dunham, for all his encouragement, and for putting me on the trail.

Gail Ranstrom, who told me it's all about the story and the voice.

Diane Manila Miller, for her truth, her honesty, and her words.

Leticia Gomez, who took a chance on us, a candle in the darkness.

John Koehler, for his sense of humor.

Joe Coccaro, for his great eye.

Donald Barton, Esq., for all the sage advice.

ICM, for giving up on me.

Jose, my jail keeper in Algeciras, for all the extra oranges—
Gracias.

And to all the writers of all the rejection letters I've received over the years, my gratitude.